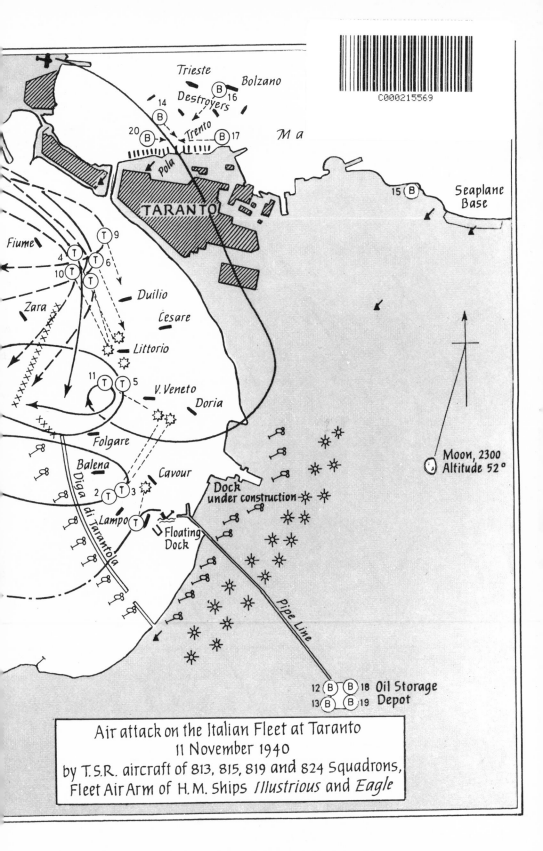

Air attack on the Italian Fleet at Taranto
11 November 1940
by T.S.R. aircraft of 813, 815, 819 and 824 Squadrons,
Fleet Air Arm of H.M. Ships *Illustrious* and *Eagle*

TARANTO 1940

By the same author

THE MAN WHO DISOBEYED: Sir Horace Smith-Dorrien and
his Enemies

SIR JOHN MONASH

THE KAFFIR WARS 1779–1877

TOBY: A Real-life Ripping Yarn

DORNFORD YATES: A Biography

COMBINED FORCES

A NEW EXCALIBUR: The Development of the Tank
1909–1939

RUDE MECHANICALS: An account of Tank maturity during
the Second World War

HONOURABLE CONQUESTS: An Account of the Enduring
Work of the Royal Engineers throughout the Empire

CAMBRAI: The First Great Tank Battle 1917

THE FIGHTING NATION: Lord Kitchener and his Armies

TARANTO 1940

'A Glorious Episode'

by

A. J. SMITHERS

LEO COOPER
London

First published in Great Britain in 1995 by
LEO COOPER
190 Shaftesbury Avenue, London WC2H 8JL
an imprint of
Pen & Sword Books Ltd,
47 Church Street,
Barnsley, South Yorkshire S70 2AS

A CIP record for this book is available from the British Library

ISBN 0 85052 491 1

Typeset in 11/12½pt Linotype Sabon
by Phoenix Typesetting, Ilkley, West Yorkshire

Printed at Redwood Books, Trowbridge, Wiltshire.

CONTENTS

Acknowledgements   vii
Introduction   1
Chapter 1   The Navy Eternal   7
Chapter 2   Change And Decay   30
Chapter 3   The Navy's New Sword   47
Chapter 4   'Some day we're bound to sight the enemy'   57
Chapter 5   Appreciating The Situation   78
Chapter 6   Dramatis Personae   82
Chapter 7   Judgment Delivered   96
Chapter 8   Debits and Credits   118
Chapter 9   'The Furious German Comes'   126
Chapter 10   Revenge, Italian Style   135

Appendix I   Some particulars of the Fairey Swordfish   139
Appendix II   Fleet Air Arm officers who took part in the
               Taranto raid but did not survive the Second
               World War   141
Appendix III   A brief comparison of Taranto with Pearl
               Harbor   143
Bibliography   145
Index   147

ACKNOWLEDGMENTS

An outsider with no more than an outsider's knowledge who attempts to write of operations carried out by the Fleet Air Arm must do so at his peril. I have been given far more help from the inside than I had any right to expect. Firstly, Mr Richardson of the Fleet Air Arm Museum at Yeovilton has been more than generous in furnishing me not only with information for which I had asked but much more besides; as often as not information that I did not know to exist. My debt to him and to Charles Stirling, himself formerly of the Museum, is something that I gratefully acknowledge. It was Mr Richardson again who took the risk of introducing me to one of the six gentlemen left who have first-hand experience of the exploits that make up the substance of this book. Lieutenant-Commander J.W.G. Wellham, DSC, RN (ret'd), himself the author of that splendid book *With Naval Wings*, is one of the Taranto Forty; he has, with great kindness and forbearance, gone to much trouble over answering questions, many of which must have seemed rather silly. In addition he generously assumed the burden of reading my typescript and red-inking it as it deserved. That, of course, does not imply that he bears the slightest responsibility for the contents of this book or any part of them.

My old and valued friends at the Imperial War Museum, Roderick Suddaby and Nigel Steel, were once more at pains to find for me everything in their Department of Manuscripts that bears upon this story and I am as grateful as I was on the first occasion, now long ago. His Excellency the Italian Ambassador was good enough to put me in touch with the *Ufficio Storico della Marina Militare* in Rome and I am much beholden to the officials there for finding the information needed about the other side of the hill. Mr McGowan, Archivist to the Royal Naval College at Greenwich, having ascertained that his sources lacked the information I requested, was good enough to suggest that I wrote to the Naval Historical Branch in Whitehall. I did. Twice. My letters were not answered.

Once again it is a pleasure to be able to put on record my debt to Philippa Arnott. Furnished with a heap of rudely-typed, much amended, A4 manuscript paper she has the rare ability, assisted now by some piece of up-to-date machinery beyond my understanding, to turn it into something almost beautiful. At any rate to this author's eye.

'For what we are about to receive, thank God and the British Navy'

Grace at the author's prep school
(and that of many others) 1920s.

'I have some news for the House. It is good news. The Royal Navy has struck a crippling blow at the Italian fleet . . . I felt it my duty to bring this glorious episode to the immediate notice of the House.'

The Prime Minister
13 November, 1940

'Just before the news of Taranto the Cabinet were rather down in the dumps; but Taranto had a most amazing effect upon them.'

Letter, Admiral Sir Dudley Pound to
Admiral Sir Andrew Cunningham

'*Illustrious* manoeuvre well executed.'

Signal from Admiral Cunningham
12 November, 1940

INTRODUCTION

The season of autumn brings with it the greatest annual number of Service dinners and luncheons. Armistice Day, regrettably down-graded in this of all countries, must forever stand apart. Trafalgar Day has attained respectable antiquity. Cambrai Day, celebrated by the successors to the Tank Corps of 1917, is on the way to doing the same, for few of the combatants can still be with us. Since the Second World War another name of power has been added. On, or near to, 12 November the Fleet Air Arm dines ceremonially in order to remember its own greatest of days. It is pleasant to know that there are still living among us gentlemen who made their contributions to that victory.

The torpedo – it got its name from a fish that gives electric shocks – had been around since the time of the Franco-Prussian war and Mr Whitehead has had many imitators. His compressed-air-driven machine reached something like perfection before the Kaiser's war, notching up speeds in the order of 30 knots. Inevitably, it was detested by the established navies, for it was, beyond argument, the means by which a very small ship could sink a very big one with a single blow. The only mitigating factor was that the upstart menace was ruinously expensive and only rich nations could afford it.

The weapon was a very sophisticated piece of Victorian machinery. From nose to tail it comprised the pistol, fitted with a safety device to prevent explosion before the due time, the warhead, the air chamber, the balance chamber worked by float and spring to ensure keeping proper depth, the propelling machinery and gyroscope, the buoyancy chamber, two contra-rotating screws and, finally, the tail. Such complication does not come cheaply. The torpedo was, of course, designed to be fired from

1

one ship to another and not to withstand the rough usage of being dropped from a flying-machine. When the Wright brothers or their associates wished to make their aeroplane into a weapon of war it would have to use the cruder and, for a long time to come, far smaller bomb. In 1914 this meant something that could be picked up in one hand and tossed over the cockpit side. Though Captain Guidoni may not have wholly realized what he had done, he had completely altered the shape of sea warfare in the future. In 1911, still the distant future.

The story begins in the summer of 1911, one of the hottest of the century. At home a new King, trained to the sea, and his Queen were being crowned with all the ancient panoply. Their dock-yards, and those of their cousin of Germany, were clanging day and night as the rivetters put together some of the biggest battle-ships ever built and experts of one kind and another devised plans for blowing them all out of the water. The best way, everybody agreed, was to provide your ship with guns bigger and further-ranging than anything that your enemy could manage, for such was the tradition of all navies since gunpowder had come in. There were other methods. The floating or moored mine – con-fusingly called a torpedo in its early days – had been in service since the Crimean War. It was not highly regarded, for it was the weapon of the weaker power, but there was no denying its use-fulness as a means of defence. Then there was the torpedo, properly so called.

There is a certain irony about the fact that it was a weapon invented by an Englishman, trained in the building of railway stations but employed by an Austrian shipyard in Fiume, who put it through its first trials at the head of the Adriatic. Mr Whitehead's torpedo, surprisingly like its descendants in appearance, was bought for the Royal Navy in 1871 and in time became respectable.* For

---

* The compressed-air driven torpedo was a by-product of the Alpine tunnels. When, in 1859, the engineers Grattoni, Grandis and Sommelier began to drive their shaft under Mont Cenis it soon became apparent that steam was not a suitable medium for the working of their drills. Recourse was then had to William Mann's 1829 invention and compressed air was set to work. The fact that it took all of 13 years was due to wars rather than mechanical difficulties. Compressed air, highly successful, became the modish thing of the late 1860s. Mr Whitehead, just down the road from Mont Cenis, was in an ideal position to learn all about it.

(continued over)

doubtless excellent reasons it was known as a 'Mouldy' and Torpedo Lieutenants spoke on equal terms with Gunnery Lieutenants. All the same, the Royal Navy had no long record of leaping at new things.

It was the Austrian Navy that first equipped its ships with the weapon. One needs to be more than middle-aged to remember not merely that there once was an Austrian Navy but that it was a very good one. Neither Austria nor Britain, however, tolled the bell or fired minute guns for battleships in 1911. It was an officer in the Italian service, Captain Guidoni, who dropped the first torpedo from an aircraft, an 80-hp Maurice Farman, at almost exactly the moment that Italy's proud new battleship the *Conte di Cavour* was being launched. The coincidence is unlikely to have struck anybody, at least until another 29 years had passed.

Since the beginning of this century a tradition has grown up that the British services, even including the Royal Navy, begin their wars with weapons that are either obsolete, worn-out, badly designed, badly made or some combination of all of these. There are, of course, exceptions; were it otherwise the swastika would have been flying over Windsor Castle these many years. The theme of this book is how a country, learning less from its 1918 victory than its enemy did from defeat, persuaded or affected to persuade itself that times had not changed and that the Mediterranean Fleet was as powerful and invulnerable as it looked; of how it fared in a later world, deprived of air power and faced with an enemy on his home ground and with a fleet at least as big. It attempts to tell of how a couple of score of officers, one a Royal Marine, flying in aircraft that seemed to belong to an age that was past, altered the balance of sea power in a matter of minutes by an exploit used for the first time in the history of warfare but soon to become dominant in everything. It tells of what

In civil life it achieved even more than anybody expected, from propelling now long-forgotten railways to making a start on Colonel Beaumont's Channel Tunnel. Torpedoes apart, compressed air proved to have little military value. The great pneumatic gun, installed at Dale Fort by Pembroke Dock, cost a fortune with its elaborate machinery designed to make the firing of a shell filled with the newly-invented dynamite a practical proposition. For all the money lavished on it the thing failed (says Sir Charles Callwell in his *Stray Recollections*) 'to provide sufficient biff'. And that was that.

happened to them in the months that followed, of the arrival of the German Air Force in the Middle Sea and of the adventures of a handful of others who had thought out and carried through a more economical method of disposing of capital ships without fuss.

Taranto pointed a lesson. Whatever might be said by any sort of expert, the Royal Navy had demonstrated that a first-class fleet anchored in a first-class naval base, could be attacked from the air and badly mauled. The successful operation was to be repeated once more only, almost exactly a year later. At Pearl Harbor.

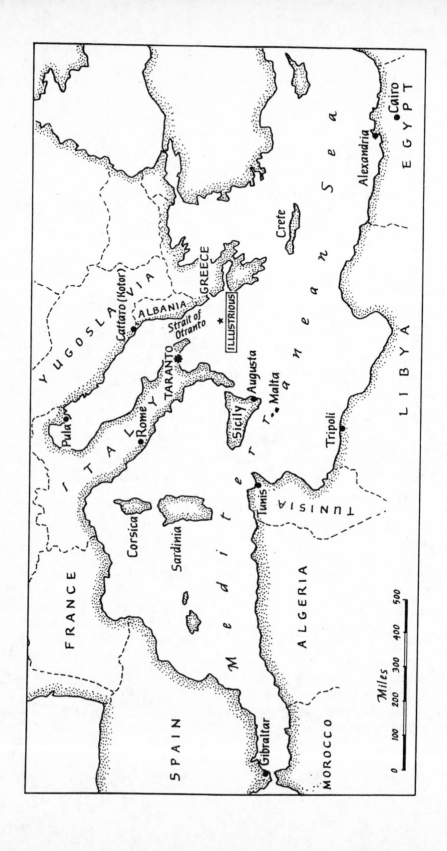

I

THE NAVY ETERNAL

Between the warm pre-war summer of 1914 and the bitter winter that followed the end of Hitler's war two distinguished naval officers, each of them a born observer as well as an accomplished writer, commanded huge readerships for their books about the service in which they had grown up. Both were old *Britannia* cadets; the senior, Henry Taprell Dorling, had first gone aboard her in 1897 (the same year as Cadet A.B. Cunningham), to be followed by Lewis Anselm da Costa Ricci in 1904. The former, by 1918 a post-Captain with a DSO, took the pen-name of 'Taffrail' and specialized in yarns of adventure with a strong senior service flavour; as 'Bartimaeus', Captain (S) Sir Lewis Anselm Ritchie, later Press Secretary to the King, wrote what for want of a better word may be called essays, drawing from his own experience to produce sketches of naval life as seen from wardroom or gun-room.

In 1918, with the Kaiser's War far from over, he brought out a book of such stories under the title of *The Navy Eternal*. It begins on a summer afternoon in or about the year 1905. Half a dozen cadets from the newly opened college at Dartmouth are lazily rowing a gig up Mill Creek where they make the boat fast and discuss their own respective professional futures. Opinion is sharply divided about the best course to set. The first, fascinated by such things as tides and mudbanks, elects for submarines. The second, after announcing that submarines are a failure, speaks of flying-machines and dropping bombs over an enemy's country. He is promptly taken to task and told that he would never be allowed to kill women and children, though who would stop him

7

seemed uncertain. No 3 takes the view that the sea should be good enough for anybody. 'I'm going to be captain of a destroyer. Thirty knots at night, my boy! Upper deck torpedo tubes and all that.' 'I'd blow you out of the water with a 12-inch gun,' chips in No 4. 'Gunnery is going to save this country if ever we have a war. That's why gunnery lieutenants get promoted quickly.' Talk drifted to mines and their sweeping until the tide turned and it was time to go. Then the last cadet spoke. 'Wouldn't it be a rum thing if there were a war some day and we were all in it? . . . Submarine, aeroplane, destroyer, minelayer, minesweeper, battleship. . . . I'd like to be in a cruiser, a big cruiser scouting ahead of the Fleet. You'd get more excitement there than anywhere. It'd be the fore-front of the battle.' How the cadets agree that they would 'meet afterwards and have a blow-out somewhere ashore and talk about our experiences' and how it all comes about is splendid reading even after three-quarters of a century or more. But there is no room for it here.

Their Navy was certainly changing, but it was in no great hurry to jettison all the excellent things handed down from Drake, to Blake and to Nelson. There the line stopped, for there had been no great sea battle since Trafalgar. Weapons of the weaker power, such as mines and torpedoes, were not the weapons of gentlemen but the Navy had grudgingly accepted them. Rear-Admiral Sir Christopher Cradock, one of the last Captains of the old *Britannia* before she was condemned and supplanted by the College, wrote of them in 1908. 'A boat once fired a torpedo. It was considered lost. For the whole day they searched and then returned to harbour sorrowfully. Then they found it had never left the tube; and Whale Island whispered, "I thought your service never had mis-fires". After that we sent them the motto of the Submarine Service, worked in silk on a cloth of gold. "Guns is Dead".' They were not; not yet. It was the guns of von Spee's squadron that sent Sir Christopher and most of his old ships to the bottom off Coronel. And for years to come navies reckoned up their battleships as the visible sign of their power.

The writing was on the wall but in invisible ink. In 1858 Professor Holmes had successfully demonstrated the magneto-electric light ('the most brilliant artificial light yet produced') and the South Foreland Lighthouse shone out as never before. For all

that, nobody would heavily criticize our ancestors for not immediately demanding that all their gas and oil lamps be instantly
scrapped. So it was in naval affairs. Between the first real flights
of the heavier than air machine and 4 August, 1914, there had
been activity, some frenzied but more rather languid, in ascer-
taining, first, whether the aeroplane had really come to stay and,
if so, how could navies best use it. In this country the directing
mind, for neither the first nor the last time, was that of Winston
Spencer Churchill, First Lord of the Admiralty; his skilled artisans
were the three brothers Oswald, Eustace and Horace Short, all of
whom operated from the marshes of the Isle of Sheppey hard by
Sheerness and, later on, Thomas Octave Murdoch Sopwith. The
official Director was that strange man, Captain – in due course
Rear-Admiral – Murray Sueter. Sueter was a man of many talents
but not afflicted by an excess of modesty. He managed by some
obscure mental process to persuade himself, a few years later on,
that he had invented the tank and had written to the King practically demanding a decoration for doing so. He was promptly put
on half pay and, in 1921, took vengeance by becoming an MP. In
1911, however, he was still a useful naval officer.

The flying-machine, in the shape of aeroplane, seaplane or flying boat, was quickly perceived as something with a future, even
if the nature of it was still a little obscure. One purpose was
obvious. Battleships, even Fisher's Dreadnoughts, did not shoot
very well. When eight of them, anchored, had bombarded
Alexandria in 1882 they had fired 3,000 rounds at the Egyptian
forts. Ten of them scored hits. Sir Percy Scott had taken matters
in hand but as ranges grew longer the difficulties of observing
where the shells were falling increased. This was the first task for
airmen. Let them spot effectively and report back what they saw
and the big gun would be king once more. One might have
expected that a service whose whole long history had been
devoted to the attack in all circumstances would have been the
first to study how the torpedo might be launched from the air. It
was not. As everybody with an interest in the subject knows,
Commander Charles Sampson of the Royal Navy made a successful take off from a makeshift flight deck rigged up on board
HMS *Africa* in December, 1911. The interested will also recall
how the first landing on board a ship had been effected by an

American airman earlier in the same year when Eugene Ely came safely down on to a similar contraption over the stern of USS *Pennsylvania*. For flying men, especially naval flying men, 1911 had been what the ancient Romans had called a year to be marked with a white stone.

It certainly introduced to the subject a character of the first and most enduring importance. Winston Churchill, once of the 4th Hussars, veteran of Omdurman, the North-West Frontier, Cuba and South Africa, had seen much of war. His greatest hours still lay far in the future but it is worth while examining how he saw himself during a previous incarnation. He wrote of 1911 and the years that followed it with authority and enthusiasm; 'Except for the year 1916, I was continually in control of one or other branch of the Air Service during the first eleven years of its existence. From 1911 to 1915 I was responsible at the Admiralty for the creation and development of the Royal Naval Air Service; from July 1917, to the end of the War, I was in charge of the design, manufacture and supply of all kinds of aircraft and air material needed for the War; and from 1919 to 1921 I was Air Minister as well as Secretary of State for War. Thus it happens to have fallen to my lot to have witnessed and to some extent shaped in its initial phases the whole of this tremendous new arm, undoubtedly destined to revolutionize war by land and sea, and possibly in the end to dominate or supersede armies and navies as we have known them.'

This appears to have represented the thinking of Mr Churchill along with other well-informed gentlemen during the period of record piling upon record that followed the end of hostilities. Before they began he had been the *beau idéal*, almost still the *sabreur* though rising 40, of a modern First Lord of the Admiralty. Inevitably, though the Royal Navy possessed no more than half a dozen aeroplanes, about the same number of pilots, and 'flying for war purposes was a sphere about which only the vaguest ideas existed', Major Churchill, by then of the Oxfordshire Hussars (Yeomanry), was determined to add something more to that wonderful year. He was going to be a flyer himself, and it is doubtful whether any successor in his high office ever addressed himself to the subject with such zeal. He shared the grief with friends of the many promising young men who died before their time, coming down as do rocketing pheasants before the guns. Undaunted he took his seat in a seaplane (the word he reckoned himself to have coined)* early in 1912 alongside Commander Spencer Gray† and, after putting imagination in its place, drank in 'the glorious sensations of flying'. Thereafter there was no holding him. His flying companions, for the most part, did not see old age; the First Lord, however, undismayed, caused to be designed a machine in which pilot and pupil could sit side by side, taking control alternately. In it 'I made many delightful flights' and a Minister so air-minded was exactly what both Service and country needed at this highly important moment. He brought Gustave Hamel, probably the most accomplished pilot of his day, to England in order that he might demonstrate how to extricate oneself from the usually fatal spin and to show how small and low-powered machines could perform unbelievable manoeuvres. Old Admiral Fisher was fond of remarking that the British Navy always travels first class, and so it was. The best of such machines as were then to be had found their way to the Royal Naval Air Service.

In the nature of things, it was not only in these islands where air power in its various forms was being studied. With machines that were barely capable of carrying aloft much more than the pilot nobody seriously considered the possibility of lifting much more than the pilot and his companion. The ordinary naval torpedo weighed something like half a ton; its intricate propulsion system was easily damaged and it demanded launching at a precise angle in order to perform its office. Before the famous 1911 summer was out Captain Guidoni, of the Regia Aeronautica,

* The word did not catch on immediately. In 1913 came 'The Great Waterplane Race', in which H.G. Hawker, the only entrant, nearly managed a circuit of the kingdom but fell into the sea off Dublin half way through the third day. He had covered something like 1,000 miles. 'Water-plane' dropped out of the language and 'seaplane' came in.

† Spencer Gray was soon to become one of the first naval officers to drop bombs on the German enemy. On 9 October he and Squadron Commander Marix, flying two of the Navy's only three Sopwith Tabloids, attacked the Zeppelin sheds at Düsseldorf and Cologne. Marix, at the former town, dropped his pair of 20-lb bombs so accurately that they went through the roof and destroyed Zeppelin Z9. Having run out of petrol 20 miles from Antwerp he returned by bicycle. Gray arrived over Cologne in thick mist; being unable to find Zeppelins he bombed the railway station instead.

flying an 80 horse-power Farman with a Gnome rotary engine had carried out the first successful air launch. This, inevitably, was a considerable worry to an Admiralty that, since the days of fire-ships, had winced at the idea of such unsuitable weapons coming into regular use.

Commander Murray Sueter was set to enquire into the matter; in 1913 he persuaded Sopwith to build an aircraft that would do the same thing and this it did, successfully, at Calshot towards the end of the year. Few people took much notice. It was, remember, the era of the Dreadnought and of Fisher's battle-cruisers. Navies remained master of their seas because their lines of great ships and great guns were more than a match for their enemies. Everything else was there only to make possible bigger Trafalgars, fought at several miles apart but still fleet actions. Aircraft, it was grudg-ingly admitted, might have some function analogous to frigates, in working ahead and telling the battle line where it ought to form. But they were no more expected to take part in battle than would be the scorers in a cricket match.

One man, it has to be said, inevitably saw further. When a cav-alry officer so defied tradition as to charge at the head of his troop swordless but firing a Mauser automatic pistol he must, in some minds, be capable of anything. As early as 3 April, 1915 – mark well the date as only 22 days before the Gallipoli landings – Mr Churchill had minuted to his Director of the Air Division that 'The torpedo seaplane must be strenuously pressed forward, the object being to use at least ten machines carrying torpedoes for a night attack on German ships of war at anchor.'

What followed was less dramatic. The Mediterranean was plainly more rewarding a theatre than the blustery North Sea and there was plenty of work for naval fliers there. Churchill's old companion Commander Samson was flying regularly from Rabbit Island to observe the carnage of Anzac Day and to beat up Turks as opportunity offered. The Isle of Man ferry *Ben-My-Chree*, all 350 feet length and 46 feet beam of her, had been transformed into a seaplane carrier and was earning her keep. Perhaps not sur-prisingly, for her Intelligence and Reconnaissance officer was Erskine Childers, Lieutenant, RNVR.

The season opened, fittingly, on 12 August. The ship owned four Short 184 torpedo-carrying seaplanes, each powered by a

225 h.p. Sunbeam Mohawk engine – one of the best units of its day – and carrying a 14" torpedo slung between the floats. As Flight Commander Edmonds would certainly have agreed, the first bag was not all that spectacular. The submarine *E14* had already accounted for a Turkish merchantman and left her dead in the water; the fact remains that Edmonds' torpedo scored a clean hit and finished her off. Three days later he improved on this by torpedoing another Turk off Ak Bashi Leman.

Flight-Lieutenant Dacre, of the same ship and flying a similar machine, added some sort of record of his own. His Short had force-landed on the sea with engine trouble; this being repaired, and whilst still taxying for take off, Dacre spotted a Turkish tug, turned towards her and sank her in the same fashion. It was not exactly *Monitor* and *Merrimac* over again but there lay the evidence, plain to be seen.

Something new and decisive had come to sea warfare. The air-craft-carried torpedo could sink small ships. Doubtless, if it could get at them, it could sink sizeable warships equally well. On the face of it, this was a new weapon that richly deserved much time and any necessary amount of money spent upon it. The Admirals, after Churchill's departure, took another view. He can hardly be blamed for the bitter comment in *The World Crisis* that 'The neglect and maltreatment of this scheme was one of the great crimes of the war'. Remember this, as Mr Churchill's innings is not yet half over. For the moment, however, he was back in the pavilion.

The minute of 3 April can hardly have been digested by 15 May, the day of his resignation as First Lord. Arthur Balfour, who succeeded him, had some excellent qualities, but a 67-year-old civilian gentleman was hardly to be condemned for failure to grasp such matters. He soon showed, however, that he was much more than a passenger and Admiral Jackson, successor to Fisher who had departed with Churchill, instructed him in matters needful for a First Lord to know. Some aspects of it must have given Balfour pain, for he was a friend to his younger predecessor and had actually given him the famous Mauser pistol.

It still had to be faced that The-Navy-That-Flies (Bartimaeus' expression) was in danger of getting out of hand even though it was not to enjoy any proto-Tarantos. Its duties were of the highest importance, covering the troop transports to and from France against submarine attack, spotting for the Navy's guns as they set about German batteries along the Belgian littoral and executing such air defence of the island as could be performed. All this was the charge of 'Winston's Dunkirk Circus', and it had strong enemies. Three armoured trains in Flanders, fifteen armoured car squadrons and the entire anti-aircraft defence of the homeland, mainly inspired by General Rawlinson's younger brother (ex-cavalry, now holding commissions in Navy and Army in turn) were becoming very distant relations to the Navy-That-Floats.

Arthur Balfour presented these incongruous units to the Army and on 4 June, 1915, Sir John Jellicoe set out the true function of the newest arm of the fleet. Its business henceforth would be to reconnoitre, to fight enemy aircraft, to defend from the air all naval centres, and to hunt submarines. A Rear-Admiral took over as Director of the Air Department; Sueter, now a Commodore, was to be in charge of aircraft construction.

The RNAS did all that and a great deal more. One of the most important figures of the entire war, a man whose name is completely forgotten, emerged from its ranks. From the very beginning of the making of an airborne arm for the fleet it had been patently obvious that Mr Churchill's seaplane was not merely imperfect but unlikely ever to develop into anything serviceable. What seemed to be needed was not an aeroplane that could just about take off from the water and return safely to it on the strict understanding that the weather would remain fine but a genuine ship that flew. Experiments with lighter than air craft had ended with the unhappily named 'Mayfly', which had failed to do so. Tom Sopwith had addressed himself to the matter and, just before the war began, he had produced, largely with his own hands, the first flying boat. He called it The Bat.

That apart, the flying-boat was practically unknown in England and very few people manifested the slightest interest in the thing. Most fortunately there was one exception to this. Lieutenant John Cyril Porte, RN, had spent most of his short career in submarines but his heart was in the air and his health was suspect with the first signs of the tuberculosis that was so soon to kill him. In 1911, that year of such deep significance for everything to do with naval aviation, Porte was obliged to resign his commission and to look for some means of employing what was left of his time. To begin with he took a post with the firm of White & Thompson Ltd, agents for various aircraft manufacturers, as a pilot, having learnt to fly at the Deperdussin Flying School in France. It was during his time there, in 1913, that Porte made the acquaintance of the man whose name was to become synonymous with the rapid development of flying from and over water.

Glenn H. Curtiss had won the first of the Gordon Bennett cups for racing aircraft, at Reims in 1909. The aviation fever that followed during the next few years affected the United States surprisingly little, for the motor-car was very much the thing. In Europe, however, prizes were offered for many feats of endurance in the air; the most relevant for this book was the one put up by Lord Northcliffe of the *Daily Mail*. It amounted to the good round sum of £10,000 – 50,000 US dollars – for the first person or persons who successfully flew over the Atlantic Ocean 'from any point in the United States, Canada or Newfoundland to any point in Great Britain or Ireland in 72 consecutive hours'. Glenn Curtiss decided that he might well be able to build a machine capable of performing the feat. Rodman Wanamaker, of department store fame, agreed to put up the money and in December, 1913, work began. Porte, 'a tall, congenial fellow', was already in America on behalf of White & Thompson, who had been acting as the British agents for Curtiss's company, and joined in enthusiastically. He and Curtiss got on well together, for they were much of an age and were both enthusiasts. When the flying-boat America made its first take-off at Hammondsport, NY, on 22 June, 1914, ex-Lieutenant Porte was at the controls. A few weeks later he was back in the King's uniform.

Commander Porte, as he swiftly became, was the only man in the Kingdom in a position to carry out the work so desperately needed. The Admiralty took over the two Curtiss boats that White & Thompson had already brought over for civilian use; at Porte's insistence Their Lordships immediately bought not only the original America but her sister ship also. Both of them were rushed to Felixstowe, where Porte was in command, during November, 1914. In all sixty-two flying-boats of this pattern, known as H4s or 'Small Americas', were delivered as a stop-gap. Having never been designed for war purposes they had their failings but they kept the Narrow Seas patrolled until something better could appear.

By the end of 1916 the RNAS was operating flying-boats of high-quality. The home produced F2, or Felixstowe Fury, along with half a hundred of Glenn Curtiss's war machine, the H12 or 'Large Americas', were something very formidable indeed, better than the Navy would have for a long time to come. The 'Large America', weighing about 5 tons, re-equipped with two Rolls-Royce Eagle engines of 275 hp apiece, had a speed of not much less than 100 mph and carried fuel enough to take them anywhere they pleased, within reason. With their crews of four and three Lewis guns they could, and did, fight off any number of seaplane fighters that the Germans might send to engage them. The bomb load of 400 lbs could be made up either of four 100 pounders or two big ones of 230 lbs. Against submarines they were deadly and their air-keeping qualities made the surveillance of the North Sea possible.

Once the great Spider Web had been set up, with the Nord Hinder Light Vessel as its centre and an intricate patrol system based on eight radial arms, each 30 miles long, extending in imagination from it, the German Ocean ceased to merit that name. Much the same thing was done from bases at Newlyn, Fishguard, Plymouth and the Scillies.

Porte did not live to see the crowning of his work. By the time the first successor to Baby was in the water tuberculosis had claimed him; two years later he was dead, at only 36. Sir Walter Raleigh, doyen of historians of this subject, wrote truly that 'The shortest possible list of those who saved the country in its hour of need would have to include his name'.*

These were not, of course, the only battle honours of the RNAS.

* On 9 February, 1987, there appeared in the *Daily Telegraph* an obituary of the last survivor of these events. Air Commodore E.F. Waring, then 87, had 'achieved the remarkable distinction for a pilot of sinking an enemy submarine. . . . in August, 1918, while serving as a pilot with No. 246 Squadron, Waring spotted a hostile submarine submerged, apparently awaiting one of the convoys in the vicinity. Manoeuvring his aircraft into position, he dropped a 520 lb bomb which detonated about 30 feet from the bows of the enemy craft. Bubbles and oil rose to the surface and it was later established that the "U-boat had been destroyed". Waring was awarded the DFC.'

The little non-rigid airships ('B-limp', their proper distinguishing name as against 'A-Rigid', gave the language an imperishable word), watching over the convoys from the West from their base at Mullion and the regular transport sailings across the Channel have their place; as have the fighter squadrons, gratefully borrowed by the Army at need, and the regular bombing sorties from Dunkirk. Further from home, the Mediterranean had been nearly as happy a hunting ground for submarines as was the Channel. The Austrian Navy is barely remembered now but a visit to the Heeres Geschichtliches Museum in Vienna may produce surprises with its splendid relics of a once highly efficient and well equipped service. The Pola base, where the Whitehead torpedo had been hatched out, maintained a squadron of twenty-four submarines which regularly slipped out of the Adriatic and wrought havoc among the unescorted merchant ships. The Austrian battlefleet, which included two Dreadnoughts, remained close at home but was very much a fleet in being. In the summer of 1916 the entire Mediterranean was forbidden to allied vessels save only those who had no other route open to them.

All this had to be taken very seriously. In May, 1915, as soon as Italy had entered the war on the side of the allies, a British squadron of elderly battleships and almost equally ancient cruisers under Rear-Admiral C.F. Thursby, had been despatched to take station in the Italian naval base of Taranto. They were not ideal for a kind of warfare unknown to those who had built them. One of the battleships, HMS *Russell*, was sunk by mines 5 miles north of Valletta in April, 1916.

More to the point, though still less than perfect, was the barrage of indicator nets laid by British drifters across the Otranto Straits, patrolled rather fitfully by French and Italian men of war. The barrage certainly caught two victims – the operators suspected more – before the submarines discovered the water to be deep enough to enable them to dive underneath it, much as their brethren were doing in the Channel. The contribution of the RNAS to the security of the inland sea was considerable.

When command of the Adriatic Squadron passed, in May, 1916, to the very air-minded Rear-Admiral Mark Kerr events began to move upwards. He pointed out to Mr Balfour at the Admiralty that all the submarines were working out of Cattaro, that their torpedoes were made in Fiume and that Pola both built and maintained them, only to be told that no British aircraft were available for such distant bombing missions. The best that could be done was to move the small naval air detachment at Gibraltar, which had little enough work, to Otranto and at least make a start. Eventually, as men and machines became available, the first dozen 310 hp Short seaplanes, complete with crews and 14" torpedoes, presented themselves for duty. Their station, built in February, 1917, on the shore of the Mar Piccolo at Taranto, was known for long afterwards as 'The English Camp'. A Torpedo School was set up in Malta at the same time.

Commodore Sueter, in operational command of flying activities, very naturally wanted to use his air power to best advantage, but the state of the art was not yet sufficiently advanced. The little seaplanes, towed on 'skids' in order to save fuel, regularly set about Cattaro and whatever ships might be there with bombs and torpedoes, but their chances of doing much damage were slight. Bad weather was enough to deter any floatplane. The spotters were far more effective, sicking destroyers on to submarines by wireless so effectively that their depredations became markedly less. The local knowledge gained was not to be wasted. At the end of 1917 Wing-Captain Arthur Longmore was appointed to command what was by then called No 6 Wing. Familiarity with Taranto and its environs would, one day, come in very useful to him; equally so to Lieutenant-Commander Lumley St George Lyster, RN, both officers having been decorated with the Order of the Crown of Italy. And each could have claimed, were he so minded, to have had a hand in the start of a revolution in sea warfare; useful preparation for what lay ahead.

These were the operations of the flying navy that it carried out from terra firma. Inevitably there were people who questioned, openly or in private, whether this was the proper function of the rightful sons of Blake and the Rodneys yet to be. There still came strange additions to the Fleet that might claim to be men-of-war. It was the German Admiralty above all that made the coming of aircraft carriers inevitable. The technically excellent Navy of the Kaiser had set itself, largely through the agency of Count Zeppelin, the task of finding eyes for the Fleet. One has to admire the hardihood of men willing to ascend in a gondola depending from a great bag full of inflammable gas in order to ascertain for their Admirals what lay ahead of them and pass back their information. It was not the most agreeable of duties; in October, 1914, the newest airship was destroyed by explosion and fire on its trial flight with the loss of twenty-eight men. The *Daily News* reported that this was the fourteenth of twenty-two such machines to have come to grief unaided.

The German Navy, to its credit, persevered. An airship, no matter how much liable to self-immolation and more at the mercy of the wind than the unhandiest sailing ship, had to be a pearl beyond price to any fleet commander; the more so when his enemy had no such machine of his own. The Navy-That-Flies, then, had two duties; it must provide spotting aircraft for the guns of Jellicoe and Beatty and it must seek out and destroy the Zeppelins. The latter task would be far more effectively carried out by attacking the hive rather than taking out bees one at a time, but the hives were distant and the seaplane's range short. A ship, any sort of ship that could be made to fit the purpose, would have to carry them to some point on the chart at which they could be hoisted out and put to work. It was not for want of trying that the impracticability of any other method was demonstrated.

The prime target, so distant as to be almost unthinkable, was the home of the Zeppelin at Friedrichshafen on Lake Constance. The exploit has so much of a proto-Taranto about it that it needs recording. The reconnaissance and planning were all the work of one man, that strange character Mr N. Pemberton Billing, not yet MP but Temporary Lieutenant RNAS. He persuaded himself, and later others, that the business could be done, crossed from Switzerland 'in disguise' and then sought out the Governor of Belfort, the obvious jumping-off place. The Governor was well disposed, the distance of about 125 miles each way not impossible and by the end of October Pemberton Billing had got his way.

Four aircraft, all Avro 504s, were smuggled into Belfort by train on the night of 13 November along with four 20-lb bombs apiece. The three pilots, Briggs, Babington and Sippe (the fourth, Cannon, had to be left out when his machine was damaged) were all destined to rise to high rank and to witness another November day in which the Navy could take justified pride. They took off at intervals, starting at 09.30 on 21 November. Their course was complicated in order to avoid Swiss air space but they flew over the Black Forest and, says Sippe's log, arrived at 11.30. He crossed the Lake at about 10 feet, climbed to 1200, dived to 700 and dropped three of his four bombs in the target area. A witness spoke of nine explosions in all as the bombs of all the little Avros exploded, and 'a vast explosion in one shed and another in the gas works sent sheets of flame hundreds of feet into the air'. Briggs was brought down by ground machine-gun fire but the others skidded over the lake and were back in Belfort by 13.50. A few small bombs can not be expected to bring about much damage but the elaborate defences given over to Friedrichshafen ever afterwards more than paid the cost of losing one machine. Briggs was unlucky, for he was roughly handled by German civilians and had to be taken to hospital. It would be different 26 years later in another country.

Friedrichshafen was not attacked again. With the loss of Antwerp it was no longer possible to reach either Cologne or Dusseldorf, both of which had been bombed earlier.

The first carriers had their chance at Christmas, 1914. Three packet boats, *Engadine* (known for many years at Folkestone as 'the luggage boat'), *Riviera* and *Empress*, escorted by a substantial force of cruisers, destroyers and even submarines under command of Admirals Keyes and Tyrwhitt set off for the country so graphically described a dozen years earlier in *The Riddle of the Sands*. The book's author, Temporary Lieutenant Erskine Childers, RNAS, sat in the observer's cockpit of one of the Short seaplanes. At the hour when men less privileged were at breakfast seven out of the nine machines carried managed to become airborne. They achieved little beyond enjoying a panoramic view of the German fleet at anchor, a solitary bomb being dropped on or near the battleship *Von Der Tann*. It had all been based on over-enthusiasm and resulted in the loss of four machines without any help from the Germans. The seaplanes were mere coat-trailers and the High Seas Fleet was expected to put to sea, though with what object is unclear. Anyway, the bulk of the Grand Fleet, lying in wait in the middle of the North Sea, sailed for home without firing a shot but not without incident. The battleship *Conqueror* succeeded in ramming her sister battleship *Monarch* with such force that both were *hors-de-combat* for many months to come.

Add to this the losses soon to be suffered of two more capital ships, *Formidable* and *Audacious*, to submarine and mine respectively, and the heretical view that there was more than something wrong with our ships seemed justified. However imposing they might look, battleships were on the way to becoming liabilities.

The submariners – 'The Trade', as the Royal Navy called them – could see fairly clearly the pattern of future war as it affected them. For the airmen there was still a long way to go before they could become an important, let alone a dominant, factor in sea battles. The seaplane was not the answer; it would do well enough for scouting purposes but lacked the punch to sink a ship save in the most favourable conditions. Nor was it any more seaworthy than a river punt. The flying machines of the day were still near enough to being powered box-kites for men to think in kite terms of how to get them airborne from ships. Boys run across the grass pulling on the string and the kite is lifted by the wind thus obtained. The same effect could be got by putting the aeroplane on a lighter and towing it at speed behind the fastest craft available. Other possibilities were the building of flying platforms over the barrels of turret guns or on turntables. All of these worked in some fashion, but they were obvious makeshifts. The only method of putting into the air a striking force of bombers, torpedo-launchers or mine droppers was by designing and building ships with uninterrupted flight-decks big enough to enable wheeled aircraft to take off and land as they would upon their customary grass fields. Fortunately the RNAS contained enough men of stature and experience to force this view upon a sometimes reluctant Admiralty board.

The first recognizable aircraft carrier was the old 20,000 ton Cunarder the *Campania*. For a start she carried only seaplanes, with crews trained in spotting the fall of shot for the gunnery officers of battleships. The spotter, in one form of aircraft or another, had come to be a permanent feature of the Fleet. Seaplanes were well enough until something better could be contrived but their limitations proclaimed themselves. Even had wheeled aircraft been able then to perform the duties they soon took up they would not have commanded support where it most mattered. When Sir John Jellicoe was told how, on 16 August, 1915, Flight Lieutenant Welsh had taken off in a landplane from

Campania's foredeck he was not impressed. He greatly preferred the idea of a home-produced Zeppelin, and it is hard to blame him.

What is more difficult to justify is the absence of this one fairly useful ship from the not-quite Trafalgar of 1916. On 30 May *Campania* received the preliminary order to raise steam for full speed, and this she obeyed. The executive order, the natural sequence to the first, though issued at 22.54, was not conveyed to the ship until 2½ hours later. *Campania* sailed out to catch up with the Fleet but her task was hopeless. This might have been, and very probably was, a serious misfortune, resulting from slackness that should have brought somebody before a court martial. *Campania* alone was something more than a mere water-borne garage-cum-travelling crane. Her forward funnel had been removed and something smaller substituted on either side in order to set up a runway right down to the bows. The time for this to be used by aeroplanes with wheeled undercarriages was not quite come but *Campania*'s seaplanes, mounted on trolleys, could be brought up from below by lift, could take off with the trolleys discarded and, with ordinary luck, return to the sea within convenient rescuing distance once their work was done. The ex-Channel packets could do no more than pray for fine weather as they lowered their aircraft over the side and watched them struggling to become airborne. One can not tell, but *Campania* had the capacity to have altered the course of events at Jutland had orders only been obeyed. As it was, the entire air side of the battle was left to the far less-well-equipped *Engadine* and it was not glorious. A solitary flight made by one seaplane that passed down a message nobody in Beatty's flagship admitted to receiving could hardly have inspired even Sir Henry Newbolt. This was not the shape of naval aviation planned by Mr Churchill when he drafted his minute on torpedo bombers a year or more earlier. *Campania* was a little ahead of her time. She steamed into history, the work having not yet begun in earnest.

At the end of November, 1916, coincident with the fall of Mr Asquith's government, Sir John Jellicoe was translated from Grand Fleet to Admiralty, with the lawyer Edward Carson as his First Lord. The greatest sea command of all passed to Sir David Beatty, from whom the public expected great things. The Navy now sprawled even wider than the most imaginative of Bartimaeus' cadets could have dreamed. Quite apart from what Admirals of the old school would have deemed to be the Navy proper there was the entire Dunkirk Circus, studying and practising the new art of bomb-dropping, with its various growths.

The Army had benefited by the acquisition of a complete and very good division of all arms, based upon a brigade of Royal Marine Light Infantry but soon expanded out of all recognition with ranks filled by reservists of all kinds. As time went by the Royal Naval Division numbered large numbers of men whose maritime antecedents were not obvious. Nevertheless, even after joining the Army and being allotted a number, the 63rd (RN) Division always asserted its individuality by speaking of 'port' and 'starboard', painting everything possible with Admiralty 'crab fat' paint and flying the White Ensign at every possible opportunity. Its foibles were treated with indulgence, for the 63rd, many of its men being north-country miners, was one of the very best in Sir Douglas Haig's armies.

The Dunkirk Circus, once Mr Churchill had become Minister of Munitions, received the best of everything as befitted the senior service. In return it pioneered the art of fairly long distance aerial bombing before Trenchard's Independent Air Force came into being and has some claim to being putative father to Bomber Command. It also became rather good at artillery spotting, again in an idiosyncratic fashion. No sooner had the Germans begun to line the Belgian coast with batteries of heavy guns than the Royal Navy weighed in against them. British shipbuilders freed themselves from contracts with friendly South American states and handed over some curious flat-bottomed warships designed to fight their battles, if any, far from salt water. These, under the name of monitors and fitted with surplus guns of disproportionate size to themselves, took station in the shallow water where nothing else could have floated and banged away with the seaplanes of the RNAS wirelessing down the necessary corrections.*

Not everybody regarded the Circus as justifying the resources

* The last survivor, HMS *Terror*, was sunk off Tobruk in 1941, performing much the same office, though her 15-inch guns were by then worn almost smooth.

lavished on it and many old *Britannia* Admirals were unable to approve much that was done by men who, though in naval uniform, saw no ships but leave ships. Whatever else their work might be, it was not seamanlike. By 1918 the Navy's business had become, in the main, the protection of convoys, operations for which an air element was indispensable. If its blimps and flying-boats could increase their ranges by being carried and launched further from home they could become the pivot upon which all else turned. A Grand Fleet Aircraft Committee had been set up in February, 1917, charged with examining the whole matter of aircraft carriers. Its unanimous conclusions were published within a very few months. Carriers had become an inescapable necessity and the need was present rather than future. Fisher's great battle-cruisers, badly hammered at Jutland, might be put to better use, but skilled labour was stretched to the uttermost and not a rivetter could be spared. Instead the Admiralty purchased the half-finished Italian liner *Conte Rosso* which could more easily be turned into something like a serviceable aircraft carrier. Their Lordships, with the benefit of a proper education in the classics, named her *Argus*, he of the hundred eyes. Though not finished in time to see service against the Kaiser's Navy *Argus* was one of the best buys any service ever made; it would be many years before her true value was to appear.

Beatty, well aware of the air's failure at Jutland, was never a patient man. He wanted a carrier and when the Grand Fleet Aircraft Committee, formed in February, had come out with the advice that one of Fisher's white elephants be converted at once Beatty snapped at it. By July, 1917, HMS *Furious*, no longer a battle-cruiser but a recognizable aircraft carrier, was in commission. The forward gun turret was replaced by a wooden 'flying off' deck, with hangar below. On 2 August, 1917, Squadron Commander Dunning, still a name of power in naval aviation, managed to side-slip to a landing on it. Five days later, attempting the feat for a third time and with a stalled aircraft, he was blown over the side and drowned. Improvements followed, including an after flying-on deck, connected to the other by ramps, arrester gear of sandbags and wire along with electric lifts both fore and aft.

Furious carried five Pups and three seaplanes. Soon she was joined by *Pegasus* with nine aircraft and *Nairana* with eight to make up the first aircraft carrier fleet anywhere. It owed much to Beatty, though some still regard his attitude over the merger of the flying services to have been apostasy.

As the Kaiser's war began to show signs of coming to an end the RNAS had taken on a very recognizable form, though it was growing further and further away from what traditional seamen would regard as their business. It was proper enough for naval seaplanes to haunt the scenes of Childers' book, avid for Zeppelins in their homes around Cuxhaven. Porte's Felixstowe flying-boats were a race apart, sinking 'U'-boats by means of bombs more powerful than the biggest of shells, fighting it out against them with Lewis guns whenever they dared to break surface and generally making the point that, in the German Ocean, it was the King's Navy that carried the whip. Other naval people might attach undue importance to Zeebrugge and Ostend, practically telling Sir Douglas Haig that unless the Army could take out these pirates' nests the Navy might well lose the war.

By late 1917 the RNAS was doing rather well. Its splendid fighter squadrons of black Sopwith triplanes were always a welcome help to a hard-pressed RFC; and it was the RNAS rather than its sister service that experimented with the uses of heavy bombs, partly as an aid to convoy protection but also as the introduction of a new dimension into land warfare. Its equipment was, on the whole, excellent: smaller in numbers than that of the Army's RFC but far better in quality, a state of affairs ruefully acknowledged by those in the know at the War Office. Herein lay the seeds of the destruction of the Fleet's air arm that was to follow. It was no fault of the RNAS.

Mention the first war in the air and one instinctively thinks of such fine aircraft as the Pup, the Camel, the SE5a and the rest; that is the good side of the story. The other side is a tale of stark horror, of waste, of mutual suspicions between suppliers, and of downright stupidity.

The heart of the trouble was in the design and making of engines. The Navy, with its close ties to Rolls Royce and Sunbeam, did well enough, but the War Office achieved a high degree of confusion by placing orders haphazardly with companies whose promises outperformed their contributions. The story is a long one, the usually accepted master-villain being the Royal Aircraft Establishment at Farnborough; the further one enquires into the matter the more one stands amazed that the flying services managed as well as they did.

There is no room for the tale here but one episode may serve as a sample. In January, 1917, the Internal Combustion Engine Sub-Committee of the Advisory Committee for Aeronautics recommended that an 8-cylinder engine, to be known as the Sunbeam Arab, be put into immediate production.

It was untried, to be made in large part from aluminium – a metal about which nobody knew very much – and warnings were given that it would be difficult to cast it properly. The Committee knew better. An order for 3,000 Arabs, taking up the full capacity of two firms, British and American, was placed. Deliveries began with commendable promptitude during the following May, just after the dreadful April when superior German aircraft practically shot the RFC out of the sky. The Arab proved so defective that it could not be used. The only alternative, the 200 hp Hispano-Suiza, was not much better; of 2,000 engines known as the BHP and made by the Siddeley Deasy company, 90 per cent of one batch had defective cylinder blocks.

In October, 1917, the month of Third Ypres, some pilots were being sent into battle in machines with French-made engines of such poor quality that the log-books contained warnings: the gear-wheels were not properly case-hardened and running should be carefully watched. This at the moment when Richthofen and his Circus were at the peak of their performance. Though the Zeppelin might not have achieved everything hoped for it had at least made the German factories familiar with the construction of engines of several hundred horse-power, while Britain and France were limited to little castor-oil-spewing rotaries a fraction of their size. The lead was never quite overtaken.

It was a state of affairs that could not be allowed to continue. After the Gotha raid on London of 13 June, 1917, the task of bringing matters to order was entrusted to a man of the rarest quality. Jan Christian Smuts, Boer General and British Field Marshal, practically single-handed, shaped the future of the flying services. RNAS and RFC would both cease to exist. The vacuum thus caused would be filled by a new and separate service to be called the Royal Air Force. It would be dominated by another soldier of African experience, Sir Hugh Trenchard, and Sir Hugh was a bombers' man. Ships and the sea meant hardly more to him than they had done to Jan Smuts.

It is hard to avoid the suspicion that Admiral Beatty, who might have put a spoke in the wheel, shed few tears. It was the Fleet that mattered, and the Fleet meant the King's ships, not ancillaries whose recent contribution to victory, however useful, was unlikely to be needed again.

The RNAS, through force of circumstance, had acquired unfriends at home. After the dreadful 1917 land battles, even more after the March Retreat of 1918, the cry had gone up that every branch of every service had to be critically examined in order to make sure that its existence was justified. Every man fit to march and carry a rifle was needed in France if the war was not to end in a German victory. The RNAS, inevitably, came under the microscope. 'The magnificent performances and efficiency of the squadrons can not be accepted as the final test. . . . How much flying, for instance, is done by the Royal Naval Air Service for the 45,000 first-rate fighting men and skilled men they employ? How many bombs are dropped? How many submarines are sunk? How many flights are made? How many Germans are killed for the enormous amount of national energy and material involved?' wrote the Minister of Munitions on 9 September, 1918, from his vantage point at Chateau Verchocq as he watched an army with victory in its grasp shrivel up. Had the war gone on through another winter it seems highly probable that the RNAS would have been whittled down to something much smaller, even as a poor relation in the family of Trenchard's Royal Air Force. As matters stood, it could hardly have been otherwise.

Bartimaeus' ex-cadets, those left of them after these years of war at sea, held their promised dinner. Later, as they climbed up the staircase to their rooms candle in hand, one enquired, almost casually, whether the Flying Man was not about to become 'a Major-General in the Air Force, or something. What's all this talk about amalgamating the RNAS and the RFC?' The Flying Man gave his answer: 'I shall be a Lieutenant-Colonel – me, what's been in the Navy, man and boy, these fifteen years.' 'Never mind, we don't care. We shall know you couldn't help being a Lieutenant-

Colonel, and that you belonged to the Navy once.' 'He'll always belong to it,' struck in another, 'he's only camouflaged and one of these days he'll come back to us. . . . The individual passes. But the Navy's eternal.'

Which is true, but the fact remains that on All Fools' Day, 1918, 5,378 naval officers, just under 50,000 ratings along with their nearly 3,000 aircraft unshipped their naval ranks and became a part of the Royal Air Force. Sir Hugh Trenchard, Bart, head of a service bent upon making all things new, was not captivated and his ideas were not those of Bartimaeus' characters. Already he had had one disappointment. London had been bombed by Zeppelin and Gotha, leaving many inoffensive civilians dead. The insult was unavenged, but only just. By October, 1918, the new service had taken delivery of its first 4-engined Handley-Page V 100s, fine machines capable of carrying bombs weighing 1650 lbs. A single one of these monsters, dropped on Kaiserslautern, had completely destroyed an ammunition factory. Two bomber wings, each with a good proportion of men wearing the badge of the fouled anchor in their ranks, were in course of encadrement at the beginning of November, one in Norfolk and the other at, of all places, Prague. As soon as the Austro-Hungarian Empire surrendered, exactly a week before the Armistice, Trenchard arranged for a train carrying a month's supply of everything needed to square the account and give Berlin a taste of its own brew. Only some days of foul weather, followed by swift capitulation in Foch's railway carriage, saved the Kaiser's capital from the revenge of the RFC and RNAS.

What happened was anti-climax. Instead of reducing Berlin to rubble the flying services melted away at incredible speed. Whether or not this was preferable to the pulverization of a Christian city already on the point of starvation by another Christian power is an interesting proposition, but it does not call for discussion here. The one happened and the other did not.

All that, however, was one with Nineveh and Tyre. Much more to the point was the shape that flying would be likely to take so far as it affected the Navy. Aircraft of 1914, compared to those of 1918, were a penny-farthing to a mountain bicycle. It would not be reasonable to expect the same feverish pace of development to be kept up in peacetime, but the aeroplane was plainly going to grow into something far bigger and better. For a start there was the Atlantic to be flown, a feat to which numbers of men addressed themselves with varying degrees of success. Two very serious questions, however, abided. Should war come again, whatever the Ten Year Rule might say, convoys would have to come again also. Would the successors to Porte's flying-boats be able to protect them or was there still work for the carriers? And in an age of sophisticated mine and torpedo, how did one navy set about another that refused to come out and fight like gentlemen? By sending in aircraft, no doubt, but how to get them there? Add the over-riding fact that nobody had any money, save only the United States, and their Lordships, transient though they were, would not lack for food for thought.

2

CHANGE AND DECAY

After the Dogger Bank battle in 1915, Captain – later Admiral Sir William – Pakenham took Mr Churchill aside demanding private audience. No naval officer of the day was more respected or better liked than Pakenham, about whom stories abounded. When, speaking of Beatty, he assured the First Lord that 'Nelson has come again', the judgment demanded respect. Unfortunately it was wrong. Even Nelson could have done little enough, sailing through minefields and surrounded by submarines. The Great War had been, in fact, something of a disappointment to the Navy in spite of the glorious end. 'The German flag will be hauled down at sunset and will not be hoisted again without permission' signalled a victory as complete as anything could have been. And yet, as was plain, no new Nelson had emerged. The honours of that war had gone to a later generation of Hostes, Brentons, and Cochranes and their names were Tyrwhitt, Goodenough, Keyes and Pakenham himself. There had been no Trafalgar. The glorious, futile raid on Zeebrugge may have singed a Kaiser's moustache but had in practice achieved next to nothing. Except, perhaps, some lessons of the 'how not to' kind.

Operations against enemy vessels in defended harbours called for the more scientific and calculating qualities of a Cochrane. Navies of his, and of earlier, days had had their deeper-thinking officers; not, perhaps, seen at their best when waving cutlasses and swarming up an enemy's rigging but rather at the workings out of bearings, elevations and powder charges. The bomb-ketch, complete with its pair of great sea-mortars, had been the weapon for this task. Lying off an enemy stronghold, properly protected against attack from cruisers and such, it had proved over and over again that ships can be sunk other than by bigger ships. Even as the tank had replaced the armoured horseman on land so had the seaplane and flying-boat demonstrated that they were the rightful sons of the bomb-ketch. The Army, anxious to get back to proper soldiering, came near to scrapping the tank; there appears to be no such word as sailoring but most Admirals took the same view. The Senior, the Rag and the In-and-Out were all in perfect harmony. Vestigia of these garage-mechanic kinds of activity might have to remain, but they must know their place. The country had no money, was heavily in debt to America and must make do with what it had got.

The Aircraft Disposal Company sold off practically everything at thieves' prices. The Royal Air Force, its take-over bid having been successful, duly took over both the old services. It wanted little to do with the Navy and not much more with the Army for it had its own ideas about the future. The Government had assured everybody – and would repeat the assurance from time to time – that there would be no war for ten years. Sizes and number of great ships would be regulated by treaty. A few seaplanes and flying-boats might be useful as winged tenders but that was enough. The view of the RAF was that of Papageno in *The Magic Flute*, that 'Everything that flies is mine'. The result, during the interesting early summer months of 1940 in France, was a firm and not unfounded belief that 'If it flies, it's theirs'.

The Royal Navy, though not the only sufferer, was undergoing hard times, something made plain by the affair that has gone down to history as the Invergordon Mutiny; more like a trade union demonstration than the events of 1797 at Spithead and the Nore, but still something not in the Navy's usual style. It did not seem to touch the Mediterranean so much. The great ships and the lesser ships went about their traditional business of showing flags and staging wonderful dances; senior officers engaged in dreadful quarrels over a Bandmaster by the unforgettable name of Percy Barnacle, while junior, and impecunious, officers were more or less obliged to play the polo they could not afford in order to keep the tone at Malta sufficiently high.

As the arteries of the battleships invisibly hardened some odd-looking craft appeared as offerings to the future. Possibly the

31

oddest was the big M Class submarine with its own aircraft hangar.* All came to untimely ends and the obituary of Captain Andrew Grey, RN, in the *Daily Telegraph* for 7 July, 1994, is eloquent of the then state of things. 'In 1924 he specialized in gunnery and volunteered for flying duties, hoping to become a pioneer in naval air gunnery. He qualified as a pilot in 1925 and served in the aircraft carrier *Eagle* in the Mediterranean, flying Avro Bison and Westland Walrus biplanes. But for Grey flying proved a dead end and he returned to gunnery.' He was not the only officer to do so. Nobody had yet attained Flag rank by way of the flight deck. One of the most distinguished of the Taranto aircrews left it on record that 'I wanted to be in destroyers, not bloody aeroplanes', even after his name had been made in them.

There were, however, some senior naval officers – Admiral Mark Kerr for one, though he had been translated into a Major-General, RAF – who continued not merely to preach but to demonstrate that sea and air were not mutually exclusive. True, there would be no more big naval air stations after the pattern of Dunkirk, Cherbourg, Felixstowe or Otranto but, they were only a part of the great business of convoy protection. In the pioneer days there had been no substitute for them, but time had moved on. Convoy protection, first against submarines with aircraft added later, could only be effectively carried out with air cover and air cover meant carriers. *Conte Rosso* had become *Argus* in 1918, the ex-Chilean battleship *Almirante Cochrane* turned into HMS *Eagle* a couple of years later and in 1923 there came *Hermes*, the first purpose-built carrier of them all. The last pair of Fisher's battle-cruisers, decked and kitted out for the purpose, brought the carrier fleet to respectable size even after the little wartime makeshifts had been paid off. There was only one serious fault to be found. Not one of them was armoured and a single mine or torpedo would kill each of them. But they looked imposing, as all big ships must look imposing, and they were joined before the 1920s were out by the new battleships *Nelson* and *Rodney*. They would have looked more imposing still had not the Washington Treaty required that they be truncated.

* In 1927 her Parnell Peto aircraft was piloted by Lieutenant C.L. Keighly-Peach who will appear again in this narrative.

All the same, these were the golden years of aviation. Records seemed to be set up with every week that passed: Atlantic crossings, flights round Africa, to Australia, the South Pole and almost everywhere else. The names of Ross and Keith Smith, Nungesser and Coli, Bert Hinkler, Alan Cobham, Amy Johnson, Charles Lindbergh, Italo Balbo and a score of others were as household as those of Hobbs and Sutcliffe. The Schneider Trophy, established in 1913, had been won outright by the RAF after some very fine seaplanes and pilots of the High Speed Flight beat all comers in 1927, 1929 and 1931.

Not far behind came the Italians who were making a considerable name for themselves in naval aviation. Their aircraft were within a whisker of being as good as those made by Supermarine and the world tour made by a squadron of flying-boats under Marshal Balbo had impressed everybody.* Germany, too, had produced something special, the largest flying-boat of all, the Dornier Do. X. It seemed obvious that these were the commercial future of long-distance flying. No aerodromes needed, but merely the kind of quiet water that most countries possessed somewhere. The never-failing Short brothers continued to turn out flying-boats of the highest quality and the RAF made excellent use of them.

It all seemed very pleasant and peaceful, the idea of a war between civilized countries being almost unimaginable. War against Italy, even Mussolini's Italy, was the least likely of all. The ties between the two countries were strong and ancient and they had no particular quarrels. Nor was their dictator hated as the other one came to be. To the Royal Navy and even more to the Army 'Musso' was one of the best jokes of the century and stories abounded.

The Italian army has always been unlucky in the view taken of it abroad. From its defeat by the Abyssinians at Adowa in 1898 to Caporetto in 1917 it had provided much innocent, if unfair, merriment. It is hardly possible for any nation to put all its males, however reluctant, into uniform, give them some sort of training, throw them into battle against an enemy whom they did not even dislike, let alone hate, and to expect victory all along the line.

* The much liked and respected Italo Balbo came to an unfortunate end. He was shot down over Tobruk in 1941, almost certainly by an Italian gunner.

1917 saw mutinies among armies other than those of King Victor Emmanuel. Italy's best, especially Italy's gunners, could hold their own with anybody. An army that could fight eleven separate and hard battles in the mountainous country of the Isonzo and end the war with half a million dead demanded and deserved respect.

The Italian navy, a late-comer into the big league, was something of an unknown quantity. Like all new members of an important club it began by conforming to rules or conventions that followed the habits of the seniors. Navies should be made up of the biggest ships a country could afford with smaller ones in the accepted scale of sizes. Italy's first sea battle, against a good Imperial navy under a good Imperial admiral, Tegetthoff, had been fought in the Adriatic, off Lissa, and had ended in disaster. New battleships had been built at about the time of the pre-1914 Balkan wars and the return of Libya to the Roman Empire with the possibility of a war with Turkey much in mind. They had little enough to do during the Kaiser's war. The main Italian theatre was, once again, in that home of the torpedo, the Adriatic. There a handful of men, much in the pattern of the pioneer Captain Guidoni who had dropped the first air-launched torpedo, achieved remarkable feats.

There was once a navy, highly regarded in the club, that owed allegiance to the Emperor Franz Josef. Its base was at the head of the Adriatic, its submarines roamed the Mediterranean lethally until the coming of the Otranto Barrage and its battleships included some of the best and most modern anywhere. Wisely, the Italians saw their role as the keeping of all Austrian heavy ships at home in their ports, something achieved satisfactorily by bluff rather than force. In the month of November, 1917, a bad one for the Allies everywhere, came the rout at Caporetto. In a desperate effort at providing the Italian army with the heavy guns it lacked, a flotilla of British monitors was sent to cover the seaward flank. Two Austrian battleships, *Wien* and *Budapest*, had bigger guns still and came out daily from Trieste in order to beat up the monitors and then retire home. 'Home' was firmly behind floating barrages, chains, minefields and all the other things a navy could contrive in order to protect its most valuable assets.

One incredibly brave Italian officer saw the way to do the business. Luigi Rizzo commanded a tiny submarine-chaser of about

20 tons displacement with a speed of some 30 knots, a crew of half a dozen and a couple of torpedoes, improved Whiteheads. On the evening of 9 December he crept into the harbour, cut his way through the obstruction, negotiated the minefields, put his torpedoes fatally into *Wien*'s side and roared off at great speed. A second little ship tried to torpedo the *Budapest*, but missed.

Six months later, in June, 1918, the Austrian admiral ordered his four dreadnoughts to Cattaro, intent on smashing the Otranto Barrage – which the squadron could have done easily – and loosing his submarines once more into the Mediterranean. At 0315 on the morning of 10 June Rizzo, in another fast submarine chaser, penetrated the protective screen around the battleship *Szent Istvan* off Premuda, launched his torpedoes and sank an even bigger and newer ship than the *Wien*.

Though highly to the credit of all who took part in it, the work of Rizzo and his crews was not something with which the naval world was unfamiliar. Similar craft, known here as Coastal Motor Boats, had been built by Thorneycrofts at Osea Island in Essex since late in 1917. It was in one of these, *CMB4*, that Captain Augustus Agar was to win his VC by torpedoing and sinking the Bolshevik cruiser *Oleg* off Kronstadt exactly one year after Rizzo's second exploit. It was not news that fast little motor boats could fire torpedoes into their betters; what certainly was a novelty, and a very sinister one, was the next Italian subtlety.

Major Rossetti, of the Corps of Constructors, and his friend Surgeon-Lieutenant Paolucci had a plan of their own. Both were practised long-distance swimmers and thoroughly familiar with the coastline from the Venetian lagoon around the head of the Adriatic. Dark mystery, after nearly 80 years, still surrounds their use of this skill, coupled with some very clever engineering work. Their target was the Austrian dreadnought *Viribus Unitis*, the pride of Admiral Horthy's fleet, safely moored behind the minefields and batteries of the naval base at Pola. The two men, presumably with official approval, built or caused to be built something that is usually, if rather vaguely, called 'an infernal machine'. It seems to have been semi-submersible and pushed along by the swimmers themselves.* On the night of 31 October,

---

* The makers gave it the name 'Mignatta' – 'Leech'.

1918, their contraption was taken by torpedo-boat to Brioni Island from whence an electric launch carried it and them to the outer defences of the harbour. For something like eight hours the swimmers pushed and pulled their machine over and around the various obstacles until they were able to attach it to the bottom of the great ship. At that moment a searchlight caught them and they were hauled inboard. Everything that followed was done with perfect courtesy. Major Rossetti politely told Captain von Voukovic that there was a bomb under his ship. The story ends with mutual handshakes at about the moment when the roar of a mighty explosion sent *Viribus Unitis* straight to the bottom. It was not Rossetti's fault that a flying billet of wood hit the Captain on the head and killed him. Nor could he have been expected to know that the ship had been handed over to Yugoslavia on the previous day. Two men and their monstrous invention had sunk a ship of more than 21,000 tons with a crew of over 1,000.*

It should have been a serious warning to any power likely to take on the Italian Navy. It was not. For reasons understandable at the very end of the most dreadful of all wars, nobody was all that interested in slightly freakish goings on in a distant place. Battleships still had nothing to worry them, save for bigger battleships. The British Mediterranean Fleet would always be more than a match for anything that any other Navy might send to fight it. Exactly the same reasoning had followed the discovery that longbows in the hands of peasants could bring down the grandest of armoured horsemen.

The contribution of Italy to the arts of war, supreme in the Middle Ages but inconspicuous for some time past, was emerging. Even more than Trenchard it was General Douhet who had propounded and forced upon his government an article of faith about the shape it was going to take in future. The air would dominate everything. The Italian General was not alone. Across the

---

* Ingenuity and courage were not always so generously rewarded. After Rizzo's second foray another expert, whose name has vanished, built a motor torpedo boat with caterpillar tracks as an optional extra; in trying to creep over the obstructions outside Pola it was spotted and destroyed. The time for such machines was not yet. Made in the United States under such names as Buffalo and Weasel, they were to become standard, and prized, equipment in the later war.

Atlantic another voice was crying out, trying with only limited success to persuade the powers that were of the truth in his philosophy. The battleship, the great floating castle, the most powerful weapon of war ever devised and built by man, could be killed stone dead by a couple of men in something costing no more than the battleship's boats.

It is the misfortune of many of the men who much influenced history that they were not always particularly likeable. Brigadier-General William Mitchell saw further into the future than did most of his peers but (like a more recent American General) his posturings and exaggerations lost him some of the influence that he deserved. In November, 1920, Mitchell was given leave to see what he could do in the way of sinking battleships by bombing.

First he was given as a target the USS *Indiana*, a ship that was old enough to have served under Commodore Schley at Santiago in 1898. She hardly made a fair test. After other old American warships had been easily despatched, Mitchell was permitted to try his hand at something more difficult.

In July, 1921, he set about the surrendered German battleship *Ostfriesland* with bombs weighing 2,000 lbs – far bigger than any others then in use – and, not surprisingly, she sank. The US Navy, no particular friend to Mitchell, regarded this as cheating. In September of the same year it was the *Alabama*, another old battleship and in 1923 the *Virginia* and the *New Jersey* that were offered up as sacrifices in the same fashion.

The last target, the much stronger hull of the uncompleted USS *Washington*, provided more resistance and was not easily sunk. This gave the Navy reason to believe what all Navies wanted to believe, namely that battleships had nothing to fear from bombers. Torpedoes, probably less familiar to soldiers, had played no part in Mitchell's tests. Before another year was out he had quitted the scene, convicted by court-martial for his part in the loss of the airship *Shenandoah*.

One can not but wonder whether Mitchell might not have gone further had he been less disliked. Be that as it may, the official doctrine became almost carved in letters of stone. Battleships, properly built, maintained and manned, had nothing much to fear from aircraft. One must assume that news of Mitchell's downfall had reached Italy and that Admiralties tended to think alike all round the world. Before long two fine battleships, to be called *Vittorio Veneto* and *Littorio* were laid down in the yards of Italy: ships as powerful as any in the British Mediterranean Fleet and twenty years younger.

The eclipse of Mitchell, however, ended nothing. The Morrow Board came down heavily against the creation of an American RAF and left the older services to arrange matters of aviation in their own ways. So far as it was a matter for the US Navy another Board, chaired by Admiral Montgomery Taylor, demanded the presence in the Fleet of aircraft carriers for 'scouting and offensive operations at a distance from the battle line'. And Annapolis took to naval aviation with an enthusiasm not seen at Dartmouth. The generation that was on the way out had good traditional views about ships and the sea. The young men knocking at the door were far less certain, but they lacked any clear doctrine. At any rate, for the time being.

The American equivalent of Mr Churchill's 'Buck and Dodder Club' may have lambasted Mitchell in much the same way as bowmen had lambasted the first arquebusiers, but there were other opinions. In 1920 there were no carriers but British carriers. The wranglings over the Washington Treaty had demonstrated that America was determined to be top dog at sea, a state of affairs that should have worried nobody. If there was anything in this carrier business then Uncle Sam must find out. The collier *Jupiter* was purchased in 1921, to become, a year or so later, the USS *Langley*, commissioned as a carrier and re-classified in 1936 as a seaplane tender.

Admiral Moffett, who died in the wreckage of the airship *Akron* in 1933, led naval aviation across the Atlantic into proper courses, courses followed by his successor Admiral Ernest J. King. Leroy Grumman, once a Navy pilot, set up his factory on Long Island and produced the famous series of aircraft that bore his name, and for which the Fleet Air Arm was to become grateful. The merits of dive-bombing, unappreciated on this side of the Atlantic, came to be understood and practised against the day when Japan might go berserk and try its luck in the Pacific. Preparations for this act of madness had been much helped by the 'British Aviation Mission to the Imperial Japanese Navy' of 1921, which helped to train the Japanese naval airmen and had much to do with the designing of *Hosho*, the first Japanese carrier, launched in November of the same year. The Sempill Mission, as it was called, brought back nothing in return, though the Japanese persevered once their instructors had gone home. In 1933 Lieutenant, later Rear-Admiral, George Ross, RN, was Assistant Naval Attaché in Tokyo where he came across strong evidence of the existence of a huge 24-inch oxygen-powered torpedo that was streets ahead of anything known to the Royal Navy. It can hardly be necessary to recall how the 'Long Lance' torpedo was to come close to dominating the war in the Pacific a few years later. Ross reported his find to the Admiralty; he was told that Their Lordships reckoned the existence of such a weapon to be unlikely. There was nothing more that he could do.

It was fortunate that the United States Navy, though lacking any torpedo comparable with the 'Long Lance', pressed on with the creation of a carrier fleet even through the years of the Great Depression. *Lexington* and *Saratoga*, probably the two most important ships in the entire Pacific Ocean, had begun life in 1916 as battle-cruisers, much as had *Furious* and *Glorious*. With the Navy Department completely in charge of its own air arm it became possible to equip the carriers with some of the best aircraft then made. Or so it was thought until 7 December, 1941.

Mr Churchill, a man as knowledgeable in these matters as any then breathing, publicly in newspaper articles adhered to the traditional doctrine. The Balfour Sub-Committee of 1923 had given as its considered opinion that 'A fleet, whether protected by aircraft carried in its own ships or not, could defend itself adequately against air attack'. This, asserted the Former Naval Person, was no more than sober truth. It is hard to believe that the man who, only a few years before, had imperiously demanded that whole squadrons of torpedo-carrying aircraft be unleashed against enemy surface ships should have swung so dramatically the other way. Nevertheless he wrote on 13 May, 1937, 'I do not myself believe that well-built modern warships, properly defended by armour and anti-aircraft guns, especially when steaming in company, are likely to fall a prey to hostile aircraft. Battleships which are built to stand the plunging fire of the heaviest cannon should also be able to endure the bombs of aeroplanes. . . . In attacking a British fleet they would be flying into a concentration of anti-aircraft gunnery unequalled in quality and in quantity. This and many other features have led the British Admiralty and all other Admiralties to believe that the battleship, and the power to draw out a superior line of battle, still constitute the only trustworthy foundation of sea power. This, if true, is of the highest importance to the British Empire and the United States, each of which possesses a battle fleet superior to the battle fleet strength of all the other Naval Powers combined.'

The suspicion is unavoidable that Mr Churchill knew perfectly well that this was hardly accurate; equally he would have known the propagation of the truth to be hideously damaging to a nation liable to be attacked at short notice by the pariah state of Germany. One has to assume that Mr Churchill was unacquainted with 'Mutt' Summers, who will appear a little later on in this chronicle.

There was, of course, another school of thought. At the time these comfortable words were being written the Director of Plans at the Admiralty was Admiral Tom Phillips and his opposite number at the Air Ministry was Group Captain Arthur Harris. The subject of air power over ships was one that occupied them in furious wrangles, Phillips being persuaded that the danger was much exaggerated. On one occasion in the summer of 1937 when the question of what would happen in the event of war with Italy was being debated for the umpteenth time, and 'Tom Phillips insisted that our Fleet would have free use of the Mediterranean, however strong the Italian Air Force might be, Bert Harris exploded. "One day, Tom, you will be standing on a box on your bridge (Tom was diminutive in stature) and your ship will be smashed to pieces by bombers and torpedo aircraft. As she sinks, your last words will be, 'That was a ******** great mine.' " ' Whether Admiral Phillips, standing on the bridge of HMS *Prince of Wales* as the Japanese aircraft did what Harris had prophesied, remembered this is not very likely. But General Ismay, who had been there when Harris spoke, certainly did.

Another witness, Major-General Sir Leslie Hollis, RM, remembered it a little differently. His account says that 'He (Harris) could see Captain Tom, on the bridge of his flagship advancing against Japanese convoys in the South China Sea. There would be no air cover because it was not available or because Tom would

40

not wait for it. Out of the blue would come a rain of bombs and torpedoes. As his flagship sank, Tom, looking over the side at the sea below, would say to his navigator, "Damn the mines! We ought to have had our paravanes out".'

It is comfortingly easy, sitting in a library chair two generations later, to feel pity for a man with so distinguished a past clinging to such a Stone Age point of view. It is also monstrously unfair. Phillips was an old *Britannia*. So also were Admirals Somerville (born in 1882 and thus the senior), Cunningham a year younger, Arthur Longmore of the RAF vintage 1885, Lyster born 1888 and thus a little later; the chroniclers Taffrail (entered *Britannia* 1897) and Bartimaeus, were class, if not term mates of them all. Lumley St George Lyster, then Captain of HMS *Glorious*, might well have been the air-minded cadet of Bartimaeus' story. To these men the King's Navy was a sacred thing, hallowed by centuries of victory and the nation's pride. The suggestion that it had overnight become a protector of convoys and nothing more would have seemed not so much treason as blasphemy. An archbishop, told by savants of great learning that all he had been taught to believe was a pack of lies, would have been in much the same predicament. To proclaim the battleship to be not merely worthless but a liability would have been the sin against the light.

The Army had only recently undergone a similar period of abjuration. A King's Birthday parade, a great Durbar, could never be but a pale imitation of the real thing without line upon line of horsemen with swords and lances galloping past in clouds of dust. Very grudgingly it had been forced upon the cavalry generals that their only remaining place was in history books or upon moving pictures.

Admirals, by their nature, took a little longer. Nevertheless, by about the time of the coronation of King George VI even the most backward-looking of them had come to accept the distasteful truth. Great ships that had, not so long ago, lorded it over everything were now likely to become hunted fugitives, or worse, unless well protected not only by deck-fired weapons of the latest kind but by their own fighting machines in the air. And, for plain geographical reasons, those machines, even if flown from carriers, must be good enough to take on land-based aircraft with all their obvious advantages.

Anti-aircraft weapons, afloat and ashore, were wretchedly inadequate, a matter that will be discussed elsewhere. The high-angled gun was no more than a conventional naval piece cocked up higher than usual. For close defence, the multiple heavy machine gun made by Vickers was utterly useless. It required a crew of several men, took up a lot of space, shuddered so violently when firing that it could not be aimed and had a rare capacity for stoppages.

The War Office was equally culpable. That the tank had come to stay was obvious. Failure to design and build a half-decent one between the wars might be excused on the grounds that there was no money for it. Tanks were and are expensive. Anti-tank guns and mines are relatively cheap. In September, 1939, and in the summer of 1940 the Army had neither; at any rate, none worth having.

The United States had done no better. When the Japanese attacked Pearl Harbor 'The Navy's machine guns were not very effective – the 3-inch was not rapid-fire enough and the 1.1-inch was liable to heat and jam after a few rounds.' Oerlikon and Bofors were quite another matter; so, differently, was the PAC – parachute and cable – rocket, of which it is kinder not to speak. Mr Churchill remained, or appeared to remain, unpersuaded. Writing in January, 1938, he observed that, 'Since the Italian alarm in 1935 the Admiralty have had whatever money they cared to ask in order to fit all the vessels of the fleet with every kind of modern appliance and equipment. In particular, protection by guns and armour against air attack has been revolutionized.'

In September of the same year, at Munich time, 'I therefore continue to adhere to the opinion I have frequently expressed that aircraft will not be a mortal danger to properly equipped modern war fleets, whether at sea or lying in harbour under the protection of their own very powerful anti-aircraft batteries reinforced by those on shore.'

Certainly experience of the Spanish Civil War had damped down some of the enthusiasm of those who believed nothing to matter but air power; and the low quality of the aircraft supplied to the Navy would not have led to dreams of Pearl Harbor attacks. But strict veracity must sometimes be mitigated by patriotism. As used to be said in certain parts of Africa, 'There are things it is not good for a white man to know.' No man, not even the greatest of Englishmen, is infallible nor is he omniscient. 'We were assured some time ago that navies were obsolete and that great battleships, costing 7 or 8 million pounds, would be easily destroyed by aeroplanes costing only a few thousands.' Too much reliance had been placed upon negative evidence coming out of Spain. The brutal truth was that the assurance was true. And one has to suspect that Mr Churchill knew it, however constrained his public expressions might have to be.

The experiences of the Second World War by no means saw off the Friends of the Battleship. Rear-Admiral W.S. Chalmers, one of the last of the old *Britannias*, who had commanded the Royal Navy Heavy Guns in Flanders as well as being at Jutland, edited, in 1951, the Life and Letters of his old Chief, Lord Beatty. In the book he explains how 'there are only two battleships in full commission in the world today, and none is under construction. The reason for this happy state of affairs is not far to seek. No potential enemy possesses modern battleships powerful enough to threaten the communications of the Western Powers on the high seas.' Perhaps that was it.

The post-Beatty Navy, especially its younger officers, resented the lowly status imposed upon the senior service by the newest. The story of the Navy's revolt is a large one and can only be summarized here. To begin with, the carriers were Admiralty-designed and Navy-manned; the aircraft aboard them were Air Ministry-designed and RAF-crewed, with 25 per cent of the pilots and all the observers being RN.

The Schneider Trophy successes produced the Spitfire; for the Navy they merely gave 'Mutt' Summers, Vickers' famous test pilot, an opportunity of amusing himself by making the cosy little Walrus amphibian loop the loop. Summers had more serious things on his mind than playing with a little pusher machine, even one designed by Mitchell himself. He had been in Germany, where he had many contacts in the aircraft industry, and after a visit in October, 1937, he was in a state of complete depression. The German twin-engined bombers he had been allowed to see had speeds not far short of the Trophy winners, but there was worse to come.

'Diving bombing' had been known for some years, but in theory rather than practice. Summers had been allowed to dive the new Ju87, soon to be known as the Stuka, and was told of worse things being in the cupboard. It was a frightening experience, for neither Navy nor RAF had anything remotely like this; nor had they any antidote to it.

By degrees the Navy was becoming master in its own house, first by raising its own corps of observers to supplant the RAF men. This was highly necessary but it was not easily achieved. The position of a naval observer was not an enviable one. To be of service he needed to be a skilled navigator, to possess much detailed knowledge of everything to do with ships and the sea, to be during action a passenger at the mercy of a pilot possibly junior to himself and to renounce all the best chances of promotion.

The proportion of pilots coming from the commissioned ranks of the Navy increased, by degrees, to something like 50 per cent, but it was still not enough. In 1938 it was necessary to come near to ordering ten not over-enthusiastic officers to train as observers. Nobody, in Munich year, could be expected to look very far through the fog of peace. The only good thing about it was that the young officers of both services refused to inherit the quarrels of their elders and got on together admirably.

It was remarkable that the Fleet Air Arm found any pilots at all. Thanks to the Alan Cobham Air Displays, the various long-distance record breakers, the King's Cup and much else Britain had become an air-minded nation during the '20s and '30s. The old services remained as under-strength as ever but young men with modern minds turned more and more to those concerned with flying. Inevitably, and properly, this meant the Royal Air Force, the aspirant to the role of protector of the Realm. A young man fresh from school who joined the RAF as a cadet saw his ultimate goal clearly. If Fate were to be kind, he would leave at the end of his time as an Air Marshal, or thereabouts. The only matter to be settled was whether he would be a fighter man or a bomber man.

There was a third choice, by way of the excellent flying-boats still bearing the name of Short but it did not often lead to the top. For the successors to Bartimaeus' cadets there was more difficulty.

The ultimate aim was, of course, to become an Admiral or at least a Post Captain. Admirals and Post Captains earned their ranks by going down to the sea in ships and did not wear wings on their coats. It took rare dedication to persuade the ambitious young NO that there was much future in playing about with the funny little aircraft spared to the Navy by the RAF. All the talents were going into the prototypes of Spitfire and Lancaster. There was not much likelihood of the Navy ever getting anything comparable.

Matters were even worse when it came to finding those whose business it would be to keep the Navy flying at all. No maintenance ratings had been trained for the highly skilled work of servicing aircraft nor was there any establishment for their training. Of riggers and armourers fit for the sea service there were hardly any. Nobody, however hard he might have tried to see a little way through the fog, would have considered it even possible that, before the coming war was nearly over, much of the last kind of work would be done by Wrens. For immediate purposes the Air Ministry allowed some volunteers to transfer to the Navy and, very generously since their own reserves were small, lent 1500 senior air artificers, fitters and mechanics to look after both the carrier-borne squadrons and those of the naval air stations until the Navy could train up its own. Still wearing their RAF uniforms, they were to keep the Fleet Air Arm flying for a long time to come.

The carrier force was approaching respectable size, even though not one of its vessels could be trusted to go to sea unless strongly escorted at both levels. *Argus* dated from 1918, *Eagle* from 1923, *Furious* – much altered from the original – from 1925, *Courageous* from 1928 and *Glorious* from 1930. The first custom-built and properly armoured ship, *Ark Royal*, did not join the Fleet until 1938, though laid down four years earlier. *Illustrious* and *Victorious* lagged two years behind her. At the moment when Summers was making his first essay at dive-bombing the Fleet Air Arm possessed 144 aircraft in what yachtsmen call a menagerie class. Every one was outmatched by its equivalent among our likely enemies (all theirs being, of course, land-based) and was in all respects obsolete. All, that is, save one, a machine that cannot simply be dismissed as being behind its time, even if it was. It was called, in the first place, the TSR 2 – torpedo, spotter, reconnaissance – but when dignity demanded that it be given a name somebody at Fairey's, for no obvious reason, gave it one that will not soon be forgotten. TSR 2 became Swordfish.

3

THE NAVY'S NEW SWORD

Everybody with an interest in these matters knows the story of the American naval officer aboard HMS *Illustrious* as she sailed up-Channel in the summer of 1940. On being shown the Swordfishes ranged neatly on her flight deck he is supposed to have exclaimed in shocked disbelief, 'My God! You don't mean to say that you *fly* those things? They look more like four-poster bedsteads than front-line airplanes'. There was some justice in this.

Charles Richard Fairey, from whose company most of the Navy's aircraft came, had begun to learn his trade with the Short brothers back in the old days on the Isle of Sheppey. In 1915, at the age of 28, he had broken away and formed his own company; since Sopwith was fully occupied in keeping the RFC going with Pups and Camels, Fairey took over his naval side and soon became his demonstrable successor. His F series of seaplanes had been about the place since 1917 and continued to give good service for as long as seaplanes were needed. Like the firm of Rolls Royce, Mr Fairey – his knighthood came in 1942 – saw no need to depart from tried excellence.

Nevertheless things were moving forwards. The Schneider Trophy for seaplanes had been won outright by Britain in 1931 when Flight Lieutenant Bootham spurred his Supermarine S6 to a speed of 340 mph. A few days later Flight Lieutenant Stainforth boosted it up to over 407, his low-wing all-metal monoplane being powered by a Rolls engine developing something like 2,600 horse-power.

Soon afterwards the formidable team of R.J. Mitchell, designer, and 'Mutt' Summers, test pilot, were translating this into something to be called the Spitfire. The test pilot at the Marine Aircraft Experimental Establishment, RAF Felixstowe, was a Flight-Lieutenant Frank Whittle, already at grips with a method of propulsion that would, before a lot of years were out, render even these things hopelessly obsolete. Mr Fairey went his sturdy way and, on the site of what is now Heathrow Airport, his company began to put together its unlikely-looking winner. Like almost every successful anything it was the inspiration and hard work of one man, Fairey's chief designer Marcel Lobelle, that brought it into existence.

In an age of monoplanes the Swordfish clung to the old box-kite pair of wings, essential when engines were under-powered. While competitors built their machines of tight and shiny metal it had its frames of steel and duralumin, covered in Ulster linen treated with Titanine or similar 'dope' to keep it rigid. No streamlined engine shape prettified this essentially rugged piece of equipment; a well-tried 9-cylinder Bristol Pegasus radial engine complete with Townend ring looked as business-like as it was. And, of course, undercarriages made for landing on carrier decks demanded a robustness that no retractable arrangement could provide.

The Swordfish was a big machine, standing high up on legs that have been likened to those of a small oil rig, with toeholds in the side up which the 3-man crew must climb in order to gain access to their open cockpits. Though styled a 'Torpedo-Spotter-Reconnaissance' aircraft the Swordfish could turn its hand to almost anything*. The planned unladen weight of 4,700 lbs was frequently almost doubled by the weight of weapons. Regular equipment was either an 18-inch torpedo weighing 1610 lbs or six 250 lbs bombs and eight more of 40 lbs each, or four of the 430 lbs depth-charges then in common use. Smoke and flame markers, normally for finding the wind in navigation but with other uses that ingenuity might suggest, were carried as a matter of course. As somebody once observed, 'No housewife on a shopping spree could have crammed more into her stringbag'. The name stuck. Few people ever called the former TSR 2 anything

* It could also become a seaplane, with floats, at need.

else. There was a petrol tank in front of the pilot, with a small reserve one, fed by gravity, in the centre section of the upper wing. Tucked away inside the port lower one was the airman's last hope, the inflatable rubber dinghy. As figures seldom make for absorbing reading the full statistics of 'Stringbag' are set out in an Appendix.

At first glance, Swordfish was pure 1917. It calls for a second one to be quite sure that one is not looking at that other old favourite the Bristol Fighter come again. The 'Brisfit', whose opening battles were in the dreadful month of April, 1917, was of almost exactly the same dimensions and performance, carried precisely the same automatic weapons (though the observer's Lewis gun was better mounted) and was still in service during 1932 when the prototype TSR 2 took to the air. There the resemblance stopped, for the Bristol was no weight-carrier but an out-and-out fighter. Stringbag's task was to drop heavy objects, mainly in the shape of mines or torpedoes.

Her guns were almost incidental, which was just as well since they were not very good. The pilot owned a single .303 Vickers, fixed in a spot ahead of him and aimed slightly upwards. The air-gunner, in his horribly draughty rear cockpit with wind almost blowing his goggles off, operated a single Lewis gun as his predecessor had done in the Bristol. The Brisfit's Lewis had, however, been mounted on a Scarff ring, a contraption that made traversing all round possible though never easy. Swordfish had no such refinement. The gunner had first to pull up from astern a metal half-hoop, hinge it forward, lock it into position and then wriggle himself around the gun in order to take some sort of aim. The intention may have been to make clear to the gunner that gunnery was a subsidiary task for him. His main one was to operate the W/T radio behind him on the cockpit floor, having once remembered to let down the weighted wire cable that was his aerial. Stringbag was not built to fight, but had other equally important tasks.

The 9-cylinder radial engine looked a little later than the fuselage, but not much. Radial engines were pure 1920s. The low-powered rotaries, much like the radial to look at, had long gone. The Vee and in-line engines were neither of them innovations but they were nearly universal in the last years before the coming of

Whittle's jets. It had been the sturdy-looking radial that had powered the RAF's Silver Biplanes – Siskin, Gauntlet, Grebe, Bulldog and Gladiator – in the years between the wars, but nearly all of them were now gone. The reliable, though dated-looking, radial engine was no longer much used here for fighting aircraft though it survived for longer in America, largely thanks to the Grumman Company.

The pilot, having climbed up nearly 13 feet above ground, enjoyed a reasonable comfortable cockpit, the only one to have a windscreen. It was fitted out with magnetic compass and gyro direction indicator, rev. counter, 'turn and bank' indicator, and gyro-horizon. There was no fuel gauge in the early models. Later ones produced something of a curiosity. A right-hand hole in the dashboard gave access to a dial some 4 feet forward with a pencil light illuminator connected to a twist-switch on the dashboard which would light it up. On the left were the throttle and mixture control levers, a bomb/torpedo selector panel with fusing switch and a trimming wheel. On the pilot's right were the deck-arrester-hook release, a handle with which he could raise or lower his seat, and a further pump lever that could be used to transfer fuel from one tank to another should the electric petrol pump fail. A communicating hole, thoughtfully placed, made it possible for the observer to lend a hand in this tedious exercise. Opinions differ about the value of the torpedo sight, a horizontal bar ahead of the pilot with a line of backward-facing lights. The late Lieutenant Lindsay Houston calls it 'the key to success' and swore by it, as 'a remarkable instrument both in its simplicity and its relative accuracy, if you got near enough to the target'.*

Lieutenant-Commander Wellham, on the other hand, had no use for the thing. 'There was never time to use it in an attack and few aircraft had it.' Much depended on experience.

A button on top of the throttle handle was the means of releasing whatever the Swordfish was charged with delivering, whether it was torpedo, bomb or depth-charge. Intense concentration was needed, especially when dropping the first, and most important, of these. Once the button had been pressed and the torpedo had been dropped the sudden loss of its weight caused the nose of the machine to surge upwards. It was, therefore, quite essential to

* Lindsay Houston, *The Men's End*, 36

keep going straight for a full three seconds after release and, in the nature of things, the pilot would have had to place himself as near as possible to his intended victim. With this in the front of the mind and the knowledge that even the oldest Italian fighter had twice his speed and more than twice his ceiling it can hardly be remarkable that not everybody welcomed the extra attention that a torpedo sight would have demanded.

The performance of which Swordfishes were capable was as anachronistic as it was serviceable. In an age when designers went prematurely grey in eliminating all forms of drag Mr Lobelle almost had it built in, and that for excellent reasons. Whatever the books might say, maximum speed in level flight was about 93 knots; when delivering her torpedo it was necessary to dive sharply to a height as low as was practicable above sea level. This dramatic feat over, the aircraft must land on the rather cramped space of a carrier deck, far more cramped in 1934 than it would be when the new generation of ships like *Illustrious* arrived. With the stalling speed a mere 55 knots this was not too difficult.

In flight the Swordfish bewildered its enemies by all its contradictions. It was, undeniably, slow and vulnerable to any sort of purpose-built fighter. Against that, it could almost stand on its head and could certainly hang from its propeller. Probably the best demonstration of this was made by the then Lieutenant Charles Lamb of 815 Squadron when, during the Greek campaign he was attacked off Corfu by two CR42 single-seater fighters. By consummate flying, almost all of it in the vertical plane, Lamb so outwitted and out-manoeuvred his attackers that both crashed into the sea. Lamb had not fired a shot. None but the Stringbag and a pilot of equally rare quality could have done it, of which the FAA had others. During the Norwegian campaign some Messerschmitts, flying low and alongside Stringbags up fiords, had been lured into running themselves into cliffsides.

One operation that had moved on since 1917 was the starting of engines. 750 h.p. affairs are not to be swung by hand, nor was the Hinks overhead starter a practical proposition on carriers. The inertia starting system used for the Swordfish's engine worked in this fashion. Two men, the fitter and the rigger, would climb up the side of the aircraft's nose on the port side, insert a two-man starting handle and heave at it. Very slowly, but with increasing speed, the flywheel would begin to move round until its whine reached fever pitch. The pilot, meantime, would have turned on the petrol, set the throttle at one-third and squirted in three shots from the 'Ki-Gas' atomising carburetter pump. When he judged the whine right he would shout 'Contact', flip up the two ignition switches and pull a ring which engaged fly-wheel with engine. There were only five seconds before the fly-wheel's momentum was lost after the propeller had begun to turn; quick and skilful work with the 'Ki-Gas' pump and throttle were demanded or the engine would refuse to start. It was the universal test of a pilot's standing among fitters and riggers; the man who 'muffed his catch', leaving it all to be done again, was not admired.

Once the engine was running the pilot's next task was to get the machine airborne. There was something like a drill for this. Once the green light had been given, unless the sea was flat calm, one waited until the deck forward was buried, paused for a few seconds and then gave the engine full throttle. This, with ordinary good fortune, ought to mean that by the time the Swordfish had reached the end of the deck the bows would be shaking off the water and be on an upward pitch. This was far more an art than a science. Once off, however, matters became easier for the Pegasus engine, well maintained as it would be, could stand a lot of maltreatment and Stringbag was a very stable flier.

The habitation of the observer was less luxurious, for although roomier than that of the pilot it was more draughty by far. This was not helpful since the observer was a busy man. His furniture consisted of a fixed stool on which to perch in order to navigate with the aid of his Bigsworth Board, parallel rulers, set-square, dividers, pencil and spotlight; sharing the cockpit with him were a parachute to which he was clipped, an Aldis lamp, a Very pistol, a prismatic compass and the Syko box. This was a rarely used device enabling the observer to encode or decode any messages he might receive or send; as W/T silence was seldom broken on operations it served a better purpose by giving the observer's hinder parts some small degree of protection against the event, not all that unlikely, of attack from below.

1917 came back in the matter of inter-communication between the three. Nothing more refined than ordinary speaking tubes were fitted and communication between Swordfishes was by muffled torch in darkness or 'Zogging' in daylight. This last, possibly only to people who practically thought in Morse, was quite effective. An arm raised and dropped halfway meant Dot; dropped lower it signified Dash. Experienced hands found it simple enough. Once airborne a well-maintained Swordfish should have all of five hours' endurance.

Taken all in all, a very good aircraft for the purposes intended. Its sheer toughness added something never planned; take-off power was enough to bring the tail up immediately and Swordfishes lifted off easily enough at about 70 knots when fully loaded from a carrier's deck. From the far shorter ones of the makeshift Merchant Carriers rocket-assisted tubes sent them into the air like jets. Once aloft, low speed and manoeuvrability far better than any fast fighter could achieve made them hard to hit, especially at wave-top height. With the machines and their gadgetry went the men. In the Middle Ages the armoured knight and his horse had been supported by the 'lance' – not a cavalry weapon, for the word is older than that, but a team of three; squire, groom and farrier. For the first year or so of Hitler's war the aircrews of Swordfishes had much the same thing: fitter, rigger and armourer performed as the retinue of the leader in the fashion of their distant ancestors.

Like all of her kind, Swordfish had two enemies, gunners on the ground and fighters in the sky. The former held few terrors, save on such exceptional operations as the attack on *Scharnhorst* and *Gneisenau*, for the machine had an ability to sustain damage far beyond that of any other then in service. Fighters were another matter. Stringbag was never built to mix it with such as the Me 109 or even the Fiat CR 42. They needed to be kept as far as possible apart.

In 1937, when the Navy was beginning to emerge from the past, the standard close-range anti-aircraft weapon remained as before. The Vickers .5 inch multiple machine-gun, the one which pilots in training were pitted against in order to learn their business, required a lot of space, a crew of several men and gave little enough in return. As soon as firing began it vibrated so furiously that any attempt to aim it was pure charade. Everybody concerned knew perfectly well that it would shoot only very approximately in the desired direction, and that not for long. The gun's only virtue was that it was British-made and found work for British labour, as it had been doing for far too long.

Hardly anybody knew, or would have cared if they had known, that something far deadlier was on the market in foreign parts. The Oerlikon, made in, of all places, Switzerland, was a killer of low-flying aircraft. One man could operate it with ease and accuracy, swinging it round as if after pheasant. The trouble with this excellent weapon was that it was 'Not Invented Here' and their Lordships and advisers needed to know no more. They could not plead ignorance. As long ago as 1935 Lieutenant George Ross, RN, Naval Attaché in Tokyo and an officer of great persistence, had been guest at a dance given by Prince Albert von Urach, representative in Japan of the Nazi newspaper *Völkischer Beobachter*. Ross, very properly, led on to the dance floor a gorgeous blonde named, like Miss Dietrich in *The Blue Angel*, Lola. Lola, it turned out, was the wife of Antoine Gazda, Oerlikon's man in Tokyo, who was busy selling his gun to the Imperial Japanese Navy. Ross and Gazda talked guns for some time; apparently Herr Gazda's firm was producing one that not only had a very high muzzle velocity but could fire 480 armour-piercing rounds a minute. In answer to Ross's obvious question, Gazda asserted that he was only waiting to finish his deal with Japan and would then be offering a superior version to the Royal Navy. The three people concerned became friends; next year Ross, on leave in Austria, was taken to Zurich to be shown what the new Oerlikon could do. The performance was so impressive that Ross introduced Gazda to the Admiralty department charged with such matters. Gazda had, in all, 238 meetings with Admiralty officials but got nowhere.

At about the same time, and with the same result as has been mentioned earlier, he laid bare the secrets of the 'Long Lance' 24-in. oxygen-powered torpedo that so nearly won the Pacific war for Japan. He was told that it was 'unlikely'. In something like despair Ross press-ganged an old Dartmouth term-mate named Louis Mountbatten who in turn press-ganged influential officers not known to George Ross. Orders were eventually placed just before the start of Hitler's war. Little progress seems to have been made for it was not until after the fall of France that Commander Steuart Mitchell, who had been sent as Admiralty Inspecting

1. HMS *Illustrious*

2. HMS *Eagle*

3. Swordfish fitted with long-range fuel tank

4. 250lb semi-armour piercing bombs on the deck of *Illustrious* just before the Taranto raid.

5. The Italian battleship *Conte di Cavour* on the day after the Taranto raid.

6. A reconnaissance photograph of *Littorio* four days after the raid.

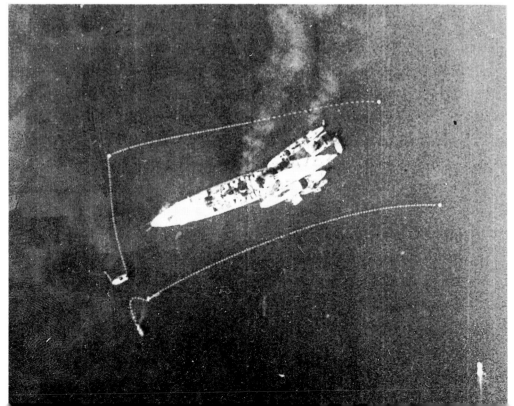

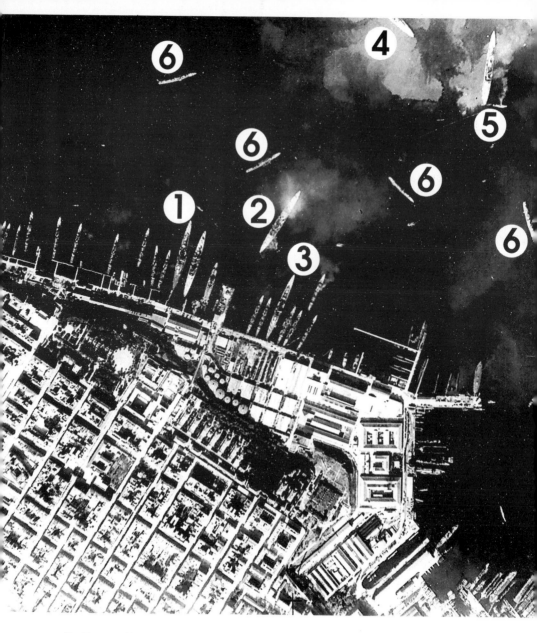

7. Reconnaissance photograph taken on 12 November, 1940, of Taranto's inner harbour, Mar Piccolo.

   (1) 8″ Zara-calss cruiser, *Pola* at wharf.
   (2) 8″ Trento-class cruiser, *Trento*, moved from wharf after raid.
   (3) 6″ Abruzzi-class cruiser
   (4) 8″ Trento-class cruiser, *Trieste*
   (5) 8″ Bolzano-class cruiser, *Bolzano*
   (6) Destroyers

Officer to the works at Zurich, managed to smuggle drawings, parts and other essentials by devious ways to Istanbul and home.

By then about 100 Oerlikons had been supplied to the Navy, most of them lost in Norway. For a long time to come the highly vulnerable carriers would have to rely for their own AA defence upon wretchedly inadequate weapons. It seems hardly necessary to set out what this must have cost during the first two years or so of the war.

In addition to vulnerability to most forms of enemy action, mitigated only by its toughness and manoeuvrability, the Swordfish, being a child of its time, had the limitations of an earlier age. Accuracy in bombing ships is best obtained by diving upon them as nearly vertically as possible. 'Diving-bombing', as it was called here all through the 1930s, had only come into being after Mr Lobelle had sketched out his design. The German machines shown to 'Mutt' Summers bore precious little resemblance to Stringbag. The Navy had certainly done well with what it had. During the Norwegian campaign sixteen Skuas, an indifferent machine but the nearest thing we had to a Stuka, had dived from 8,000 feet at an angle of 60 degrees and sunk the *Königsberg* with 500-lb bombs. Reports by pilots spoke regularly of 'dive-bombing' now but it would hardly be reasonable to equate Stuka and Swordfish in this sort of operation.*

For Swordfish squadrons to succeed against well-manned and equipped heavy ships the element of surprise, though rarely possible, is essential. On their best day, the subject of this book, it was planned but, through bad luck, not achieved. Their blackest came in February, 1942, when half a dozen were sent, in broad daylight, on the suicidal mission of trying to torpedo the German pocket-battleships *Scharnhorst* and *Gneisenau*, along with the cruiser *Prinz Eugen*, as they made their way up the English

---

* Two of the most successful Taranto aircrews, Sub-Lieutenant (A) R.A. Bailey, DSC, RN, and Sub-Lieutenant (A) A.S.D. Macaulay, DSC, RN, were killed in June, 1941, when, in the course of a dive-bombing attack on a Vichy French ship, the wings of their Swordfish were torn off. The reason was not, as is sometimes said, that the strain had been too great. It was all due to a faulty locking-pin.

The suffix (A) was awarded to officers who entered the RN Air branch direct or from the RAF in 1938/39.

Channel. All of them, flying from a field in Kent, were shot down, having achieved nothing. Their crews had expected it. But in the time intervening there was work for Stringbag to do, and work that no other aircraft could even contemplate doing.

Having been in at the beginning, Swordfishes were still fighting at the end. In all, 2,391 of them were built; they sank a greater tonnage of enemy shipping than did any other allied aircraft and it was a Stringbag that had the distinction of mounting the last naval engagement of Hitler's War. Exactly four hours before the German plenipotentiaries put their names to the Instrument of Surrender on Luneberg Heath a German midget submarine popped up in the Channel. Since it was plainly up to no good it attracted the attention of a Swordfish, which promptly sank it. Seldom, if ever, has an inanimate object been held in such affection by those who served it. Whether the American officer mentioned before came to share this feeling is nowhere recorded.

4

'SOME DAY WE'RE BOUND TO SIGHT THE ENEMY'

'Some day we're bound to sight the enemy
He's coming, tho' he hasn't yet a name'.

Sir Henry Newbolt, 'The Little Admiral' (1910)

Round about the time that the Swordfish was first coming up for testing, the world began to fall apart. Men who had been there thought wistfully of the great armies of 1918. The Navy excited less emotion, save amongst the best informed, since it still looked as formidable as ever. Hitler's upstart pocket-battleships would not fancy taking on the likes of *Nelson* or *Rodney*, let alone the newer ships now on the stocks. The submarine had been mastered by 1918 and there was no reason to believe that the cause had altered. Malta and Gibraltar remained as impregnable as ever; should the worst happen and Italian air power diminish their value then France would surely allow the Navy to use Toulon and Bizerta. At a pinch Alexandria might be used but it possessed none of the attributes of a base for a great fleet. There was nothing to worry about. Croakers do not get promotion.

It was among the newest arm squadrons that the doubts existed. When Mussolini began his war with Abyssinia in 1935 his posturings produced much mirth, but he had to be taken seriously. Italian aircraft were excellent; their pilots might have a tendency to show off but they knew their business. The British carriers were all of them little more than promising targets to the Savoia-Marchetti SM 79 and Fiat BR20 bombers which were well equipped with bombs and torpedoes and had practised the use of both without regard for anything like economy. Neither would have been equal in a fight even with Swordfish's contemporaries, the Bulldog, Gauntlet or Gladiator. The Navy had none such, nor were any belonging to the RAF available for the task. No preventive action could be planned against the Regia Aeronautica, and officers with long memories had uneasy recollections of the fate of the Austrian Dreadnoughts.

One thing could be set in motion, however. There were still people in the Royal Navy who knew Taranto, the main Italian base in the south, almost as well as they knew Portsmouth. No firm evidence seems to exist now but it was believed at the time that a plan was drawn up for an air strike on the Italian fleet there during the Abyssinian war of 1935. It would have been a pale shadow of what the RNAS could have done half a generation earlier. The only bombers available were the Blackburn Dart and Fairey Seal and their offensive power consisted of four 20-lb bombs carried below the wings. Not exactly a devastating blow, but it was the best that could be mustered in the year of the Silver Jubilee. The plan, the work of Captain Lumley St George Lyster acting on the orders of Admiral Sir William Wordsworth Fisher, was locked in the safe of his ship, the carrier *Glorious*, as something deadly secret.

Geographically there was much to be said in support of Mussolini's claim to the Middle Sea as *'Mare Nostrum'*. Historically, though, since Blake burst into it under the Commonwealth in 1654, it had been Tom Tiddler's Ground, governed by whichever of two fleets, British or French, happened for the moment to be the stronger. The Mediterranean Fleet had long been the most prized command for any British admiral, for it was a long way from Whitehall and none of the smaller powers seemed to mind in the least when the Navy made free with their bays and coasts in the name of training.

All this was about to change as a King, himself brought up in the ways of the Royal Navy, lay dying. From early in 1936 everybody with eyes to see could gain a pretty fair idea of the shape of things to come so long as Hitler lived. The march of the German army into the Rhineland was the first Armada beacon; beside this, Mussolini looked a bit-part player. Germany was the enemy and Germany alone had the power to destroy these islands. Slowly, very slowly, this piece of obvious intelligence forced itself upon a half-persuaded government. The Navy came second in the queue when, in 1937, Mr Baldwin announced his intention of re-arming the nation at the cost, enormous for those days, of £1500,000,000. It was not possible to deny the first place to the RAF, even when received opinion announced that 'the bomber will always get through'. Money, though useful, was not needed by the Fleet Air Arm so much as time, time in which to prepare itself and its worn-out gear for the fight to the death that was plainly coming and that very soon.

At the beginning of 1936, when the RAF began to return naval aviation to the Navy, there was not much to hand over: four airfields, at Lee-on-Solent, Ford, Worthy Down and Donibristle, and five carriers which could muster between them 144 aircraft, every one obsolete or nearly so. In addition twenty-nine large warships carried flying machines, thirty-four in all, that could be catapulted off and, with luck, craned back. These flying picket-boats were all spotters and nothing else, the best of them being the Seafox floatplane; it won a moment of glory when one of them remarked the *Graf Spee* and so brought about the first naval victory of the war.

The RAF's Coastal Area, renamed Coastal Command, had the advantage of being commanded by an old RNAS man, the same Arthur Longmore, now Air Marshal, who had once commanded in the Adriatic. This was helpful, for when the divorce came the Navy, though not too badly off for pilots and observers, was desperately short of the highly skilled men needed to get their machines into the air and keep them flying. How the sister service came to the rescue has already been mentioned. It was not until February, 1937, that the Naval Air Branch, of officers for flying duties only, came into existence. It was not over-subscribed. When, a year later, aspirants were sought to train as observers a good number had to be almost ordered to volunteer.

Everybody with an interest in such things knew the unarmoured carriers to be survivors from an earlier age and doomed. The fact remained that they were absolutely essential to the Fleet and that nothing else was presently available. The number of them was raised to seven by re-activating *Argus*, even though only for training purposes, and more serviceably by the commissioning at the end of 1938 of *Ark Royal*. Here at last was an up-to-date fighting ship, armoured and superior in every way to her predecessors. To match her quality the Fairey Company produced an equally superior fighter, the 8-gunned Fulmar which, though no Spitfire, could take on most of the opposition likely to come its way. The prototype flew in January, 1937, but it was not until the Dunkirk evacuation was over that *Ark Royal* received her first batch of them. The lack of pilots was so serious that in November, 1938, after the horrible scare of Munich, an Air Branch of the RNVR was called into existence with the hope of attracting young men with at least some flying experience. This it did.

Let us now consider the opposition. Germany, whether Imperial or not, was master of the aggressive war. Successfully to overcome an enemy of something like equal power a new, devastating weapon is highly desirable, and the greater the secrecy surrounding it the better. In 1914 it had been the great howitzers that smashed Brialmont's forts. In 1939, among other refinements on older methods, it was to be the dive-bomber.

Germany, with no longer a High Seas Fleet, had no plans to re-fight Jutland, nor did its navy need carriers. Submarines and commerce-raiders apart, the German fleet was a short-legged affair. Unlike the King's ships, it was not designed to operate in distant waters and its crews more often than not lived ashore in barracks. The obvious savings in space gave the naval architects scope for designing ships with far less domestic equipment but more fighting gear for their size. Gun for gun, there was not much in it between all the fleets concerned, but the Germans were more up-to-date than all but the very newest of British capital ships. Their object in life was, in the main, to make sure that the Royal Navy dissipated its strength in keeping them permanently marked.

The dive-bomber was a new thing. Originally, as demonstrated to Summers, it was an army weapon and, as events would soon show, an over-rated one. On land it made frightening noises, was ideal for scattering columns of refugees wearily pushing their prams along French roads, but against steady troops it failed, except as an ancillary to massed tanks. There comes a moment, at the bottom of the dive, when the bomber has to make its vertical 'U'-turn and hangs low overhead. Then it becomes vulnerable not only to light automatic fire but even to the Edwardian short Lee-Enfield rifle. At sea, though not its designed purpose, the Stuka was deadly; a heavy bomb, dropped with complete accuracy from a fair height, would sink almost anything that swam, and the Navy's anti-aircraft weapons, until the coming of foreign ones, were wretched.

The submarine position was almost worse. It is a truism that armies – and presumably navies – learn more from defeats than from victories. By 1918 the navies of the Allies reckoned, not without justice, that they had the 'U'-boat mastered. The photographs, proudly displayed, of them all trooping in to surrender was surely evidence enough. In the intervening couple of decades, however, the improvements that had taken place were almost wholly one-sided. The submarine was as much a menace as it had been in 1917; the only lesson hanging over from the Kaiser's war was that convoys were essential if anything was to get through.

Armies and navies are like orchestras. To be kept at anything like concert pitch they need practice. When the Civil War in Spain erupted in 1936 there was joy along the Rome–Berlin axis. Here was the opportunity to find out how far the new doctrines of blitzkrieg and the like were well-founded and an equally welcome one to give ship and aircrews the chance of actually sinking real ships and bombing real people. It was a pity that the Spanish forces were so far behind the times but there were lessons for airmen and submariners if for nobody else. Both Hitler and Mussolini were suitably grateful.

Most importantly, from the narrow standpoint of this book, the Spanish War brought trouble to the Mediterranean. It both strengthened and sharpened up the forces that would probably be opposed to Britain and France and also demonstrated the fact that their own navies were nothing like as formidable as they looked. Admirals of all countries have advantages denied to Generals. If an army is attacked by a more powerful one then its commander must do the best he can with what he has got; should his army be beaten then that is probably the end of the matter. The Admiral is in happier case. Should defeat stare him in the face he can, except on rare occasions, take his fleet home, make it fast behind its moles and breakwaters and hope for better times.

Axiomatic though this is, it would be of little help to the Mediterranean Fleet of 1939. The Mediterranean had to be held. It was the key to all Imperial communications, the main trade route to the East and underneath it ran the 'All Red' cable. The distance from England to Bombay by the Cape route added 4,000 miles to the journey; to Singapore it meant another 3,000 miles and to Sydney an extra 1,000. The British Admiral, quite apart from such considerations as that the Royal Navy does not refuse action, did not enjoy the advantages set out above. Gibraltar had no airfield and might at any moment come under fire from German or Spanish batteries. Malta was in the centre of a web of Italian air bases from which attacks could be launched at any hour of the day or night. It is less than 100 miles from Tunis to Sicily, with Malta lying somewhere in the middle. Even if the heavy warships themselves could deal with such attacks – a doubtful proposition – highly vulnerable targets in the shape of magazines and the stores which provided for the navy's needs were wide open. And there was no other naval base of the first order on the 6,000-mile passage from Malta to Singapore. From Gibraltar to Alexandria is 1800 miles; the fact remained that, if driven from Malta and without having the French North African bases available, the Navy would have to make the best it could of the only Egyptian harbour there was, even though it had virtually no air protection and was only minutes of flying time from the Italian aerodromes in Libya. Few people were thinking in terms of a land war dragging up and down the North African littoral for a matter of years. The Mediterranean was Navy business, with such help as the RAF could spare from its fight to the death with the Luftwaffe nearer home.

Almost worse was the fact that the sea would have to be commanded with obsolete weapons. From about Crécy in 1346 until the end of the nineteenth century it could have been safely taken for granted that the British services were at least as well armed as were their foes. The change became apparent when President Kruger, rich with gold and diamonds, approached the arms factories of Europe and kitted out his land forces with the latest forms of cannon, machine gun and rifle, each specimen better in every way than those issued to the British Army. It was our good fortune that there was no Boer battlefleet. The dismal story continued throughout the Kaiser's war and it seems hardly necessary to set it all out. The most relevant figure relates to bombs. When Trenchard's Independent Air Force set about the bombing of Germany in June, 1918, it carried mostly bombs weighing one hundredweight, some of 230 lbs, about fifty of 550 lbs and the single 1650 lb monster. In his 1935 prize-winning essay on the subject Squadron Leader E.J. Kingston McCloughry estimated that almost one-third of them had failed to explode. There seems to have been little enough improvement during the inter-war pause.

There was one small advantage the Navy had. With so few trained aircrews available everybody knew everybody else and the club atmosphere can not have been so very far removed from Nelson's Band of Brothers, which is not the same as a mutual admiration society. Practically all of them had learnt their flying with the RAF and the majority had, for a time, held commissions in both Services. It was hard to decide whether to be jealous of the RAF or not. Certainly they had the best fighters then in production anywhere, and upon them, equally with half a hundred of the old Navy's destroyers, depended the health and safety of these islands.

As for the rest, there was not much to be envied. Mr Fairey's Battle bomber was the airman's equivalent of a coffin ship and, in September, 1939, there was little enough sign of anything better in that class of machine coming soon into squadron service. In the short time available to them the Fleet Air Arm pilots and observers trained as hard as they could for the work that probably lay ahead for them, the attack on well-defended ships with bomb and torpedo.

There is an interesting passing reference to this in the obituary of Rear-Admiral Bolt in the *Telegraph* of 2 April, 1994. 'Although in the 1930s the Fleet Air Arm was still controlled by the RAF, and the Navy lacked modern aircraft, many war-time tactics – dive-bombing, torpedo attacks, night attacks using flares – were intensively exercised. . . . In 1980, when doubt had been cast on the quality of the aircrews who had served in *Glorious* before the war, Bolt established that those same officers had between them won 5 DSOs and 28 DSCs'. The Admiral – inevitably 'Ben' to his friends – had commanded 812 Squadron in that ship between June and September, 1939.

Again, in passing still, another quotation from the same place is not wholly irrelevant: 'In *Glorious*, Bolt contributed to the first discussions of a plan to make a night torpedo attack on the Italian battle fleet in harbour.' It was his misfortune, grievous for a man who had qualified as an observer back in 1931, to be invalided home for a tonsillectomy almost at the very moment the Second World War began. There was, however, much left for him to do, though outside the pages of this book.

For the last forty years, if not longer, it had come to be expected in this country for wars to begin disastrously. It was not necessary to be senile in order to remember 'Black Week' of 1899 and the Retreat from Mons. This time it was to be the turn of the sea services, Royal and Merchant Navies alike, in taking the first prepared blows of an enemy who was awaiting opportunities. The carrier *Courageous* lasted exactly a fortnight, being sunk by a submarine in the Western Approaches while engaged in 'U'-boat hunting. To the sea bottom with her went some 500 men and twenty-four Swordfishes. Two of the Taranto pilots, Charles Lamb and Launcelot Kiggell, were amongst the survivors; they were to form a part of a new FAA squadron, No 815.

Ark Royal was lucky not to have gone the same way; only defects in the new-fangled magnetic pistols with which all the torpedoes aimed at her were fitted saved her. The killer of *Courageous, U 29*, got away scot-free; the destroyers saw off *U 39, Ark Royal*'s molester, in short order. For all that, and for all the disdain with which everybody treated the regular assertions of her sinking made in the curious voice of the man called 'Lord Haw-haw' there was no gainsaying the fact that the *Ark*'s days were numbered. As the only carrier fit to be exposed to action she must do all the damage she could before, by one means or another, the Germans got her. Her days in active service amounted to 803, far more than could reasonably have been expected.

Whoever was responsible for the grotesque expression 'phoney war' can have known little enough about what was happening at, over, or under the sea. Bartimaeus' cadet who had wanted to go into submarines would probably have been hardened enough during the Kaiser's war to expect nothing else from Germans, but the sinking of a ship full of children heading for the safety of Canada on the first day of hostilities loudly proclaimed that standards of chivalry peculiar to that country had not fallen off. To begin with, it was a destroyer's war and there were never nearly enough of them; and far too many were almost antiques.* Soon the old names were in the news again. Once more aircraft set out to bomb the old Zeppelin haunts around Tondern and Hoyer, but this time the work fell to the RAF. At a time when even something that might pass as a very small victory was eagerly sought the film about the raid on Sylt – *The Lion Has Wings* – produced fair applause from a generation that knew not war. Their seniors, while not unmindful of the courage shown by crews of some pretty indifferent aircraft, were quieter. They guessed, correctly, that the raid had done little more damage than had the seaplanes of the RNAS. In the very cold and rather discouraging winter of 1939–40 anything that was not some sort of defeat was welcome. When the German steam-hammer hit France in the following May it was not all that unexpected, save perhaps in degree.

What few people had bargained for was a campaign in Norway, something quite unprecedented in a long military and naval history. The panzer divisions in France caught the Army off balance, though they ought not to have done so. Rather worse was the fate awaiting such detached portions of the Navy as were sent North. Air power was obviously of the first importance. Since airfields fit for use hardly existed, the carriers would have to go. Everybody knew their aircraft to be no match for German fighters based on land but go they must; and they did.

The Mediterranean Fleet suddenly found itself to be the Navy's orphan child. It served no vital purpose, so long as Italy kept out of the war, and the fleet in home waters drew heavily upon it. By the time of the Dunkirk evacuation a battleship had gone – *Royal Oak*, sunk at her moorings in Scapa Flow by a 'U'-boat – along with twenty-two destroyers sunk and about the same number *hors-de-combat* for some time to come. Sir Dudley Pound had

---

* Bottom was surely reached at the end of 1939. When the Cavalry Division, with all its horses, was ordered to France on its way to the Middle East the usual Channel packets, *Maid of Kent, Maid of Orleans, Invicta* and *Canterbury*, were commandeered. All that could be found for their protection was a half-company of infantry from a nearby second-line Territorial battalion with a score or so of ancient but still serviceable Lewis guns. It was commanded by the author of this book, then a Second Lieutenant (Acting Captain) just short of his 21st birthday. Any naval presence there may have been was not conspicuous. Fortunately nothing over-exciting happened.

struck his flag in *Warspite* back in June, 1939, in order to repair to the Admiralty as First Sea Lord.

His successor, Sir Andrew Cunningham, inherited a handsome-looking legacy. From his flagship *Warspite* he could survey as fine a command as any Admiral ever enjoyed: the battleships *Malaya, Barham* and *Ramillies*, two squadrons of cruisers, three flotillas of destroyers, another of submarines and another yet of motor torpedo-boats. Along with the usual repair and depot ships and *Glorious* herself, with the Portsmouth floating dock on passage to Alexandria which had hardly any of the necessary facilities, Sir Andrew saw much in which he could take a legitimate pride. The fact that only small repairs could be made to his ships, and those mainly by employees of Alexandria tramways, cast a shadow over the sun, but there was no escaping geography. As soon as Mussolini saw his chance and sprang, it would be Alexandria or Davy Jones.

It was a worrying time for any Admiral in such a place. Breathing down his neck were the shades of Blake, of Byng, of Nelson, Edward Pellew and Alexander John Ball, two Troubridges, and more recently of Carden and de Robeck. And the most relevant of this mighty company was Byng, especially when a letter from the First Sea Lord arrived at the end of May, 1940: 'I am afraid you are terribly short of "air", but there again I do not see what can be done because, as you will realize, every available aircraft is wanted in home waters. The one lesson we have learnt here is that it is essential to have fighter protection over the fleet whenever they are within the range of enemy bombers. You will be without such protection, which is a very serious matter, but I do not see any way of rectifying it.'

In fact the entire 'air' of the Mediterranean fleet consisted of a few flying boats, divided between Malta and Alexandria. 'Excellent,' said the Admiral, 'when there was no opposition, but quite unsuitable for work anywhere near an enemy coast within range of shore-based aircraft.'

Not that the Fleet was by then quite the same as the one Cunningham had taken over. *Glorious* and all the battleships, together with most of the cruisers and destroyers, had gone. By the dawn of 1940 the once finest command of them all numbered three small 'C' class cruisers and a handful of 1918 vintage destroyers belonging to the Royal Australian Navy. There was nothing for them to do throughout that interesting Spring but watch and wait. Not that these limited functions spelt idleness for everybody. Plans needed to be made for just about every possible scenario. Italy might very well invade Greece. What, should real war follow this, was the Fleet to do? Then Germany, with Austria in tow, might invade the Balkans. Or Turkey might do almost anything. Crete, Cyprus, the Dodecanese where the Italian airbase was supposed to be, and above all Malta all demanded that staff work be done about them. In the absence of a serious fleet these were war games, but vastly important for all that. The one situation for which no plan existed was, inevitably, the one that happened. No scheme had been drawn up for the taking over of the Navy of a defeated France.

The main thrust of the Navy had been, of course, on England's own doorstep, or nearly so. Once the German invasion of France got under way work for the destroyers doubled and trebled, nor did they ever fail. Greater events overshadowed what would at any other time have been counted as worthy of being chronicled in letters of gold. The sheer hard courage of the ships' companies of *Keith, Whitshed* and *Vimiero*, steaming into Boulogne harbour, helping out a hard-pressed garrison with their guns weighing into German tanks at point-blank range and finally picking up the last of them under the lash of half the German air force – or so it seemed at the time – can hardly have been equalled, let alone excelled, anywhere in the Navy's long history. As seemed inevitable, these brave little ships had only a few days more to live. Pound, a destroyer man to the tips of his fingers, was with each of them in spirit but he could conjure up no more.

Then there was the magnetic mine. Cunningham was faintly scornful, pointing out that we had used the things ourselves in 1918, and incredulous that counter-measures were not ready in place. It did not seem quite that simple to Captain Roger Lewis RN and his four companions from HMS *Vernon* as, in dark and pouring rain, they crawled across Shoeburyness mud flats on a November night in order to dismember a dark menacing-looking object partly embedded in the sand. One more deadly threat to everything that floated had been overcome.

It was Norway that opened all eyes to the simple fact that sea warfare had utterly changed and that, in confined waters, the latest and best battleship was of little more use than HMS *Victory*. The demand for carriers, far from ideal but the only possible weapon, went loudly up. Both *Ark Royal* and *Glorious* were at Alexandria on 8 April when both were ordered to make for home at top speed. On their arrival at Gibraltar *Ark Royal* was ordered to remain while *Glorious* went on. A couple of days later orders were changed once more and the two ships reached the Clyde at about the same time. From there they sailed to Norway to join *Furious* in taking on both German Navy and Air Force as best they could. It was hardly a fair contest and certainly not one designed for the Swordfish. Had he been there to see it Admiral Cunningham might have modified his expressed opinion that ships moving at high speed and free to manoeuvre were not easy targets and special aircraft in great numbers would be required to put a carrier out of action. The Germans had more than enough of these; their friends the Japanese were not far behind. The Allies had not. France contributed practically nothing; the only torpedo-carrier worth mentioning with the Royal Navy in early 1940 was the Stringbag.

Norway was the first example of those heart-breaking operations forced upon Britain early in this war. The campaign, unplanned and hopeless from the start, could not have been won. The men, ships and aircraft committed to it were sacrificial victims. And yet honour demanded that we could not leave a friend calling in vain for even the small amount of help we could extend. It is easy to propound the problem set before our then leaders; less so to assert unarguably what they ought to have done. The Norwegian campaign cost the Navy, along with many smaller ships, the second of Fisher's old battle-cruisers. HMS *Glorious*, along with the destroyers *Ardent* and *Acasta*, encountered the German pocket-battleships *Scharnhorst* and *Gneisenau* at 5.52 pm on 8 June, 1940. A brave attempt to put four Swordfish into the air and hit back with torpedoes ended when a heavy shell went through the flight deck and penetrated the forward part of the upper hangar. The destroyers, whose performances could not have been bettered, vainly tried to hide their charge with smoke screens but such a fight could have only one end. By 7.30 all three ships were at the bottom of the sea. Out of combined ships companies of 1474 all ranks only forty-five survived. Maintenance of honour is a costly business.

More or less contemporaneously with these events came the Dunkirk evacuation. Dunkirk, home to the 'Circus' which had played such a part in the early days of the RNAS, now stood only for an ignominious scuttle for cover. The Royal Navy, most especially its destroyers again, had much to do with it but the Fleet Air Arm very little. The carrier fleet had suddenly become very thin on the face of the sea. *Ark Royal*, still the only one of her kind, was ordered into dry dock at Greenock. *Furious* was sent to the Clyde, out of harm's way.

Then came the French surrender and Oran. The former event ought by rights to have caused dejection and fear amongst the armed forces of the King. It did nothing of the kind. Back in Alexandria Admiral Cunningham awaited a visit from his destroyer commander, Vice-Admiral Tovey. On arrival the younger man ran up the gangway, wreathed in smiles, and said, 'Now I know we shall win the war, sir. We have no more allies.' On all sides in the home country one heard the same. 'It may look pretty bad, but at least we are rid of the French and can do things our own way.'

Agreeable though the thought was, there was no denying that affairs in the Mediterranean, the direction in which the war was now tending, could hardly have looked blacker. The eliminating of the French fleet, sentiment apart, had provided useful experience and with it further proof of the power of well handled torpedo-bombers. *Ark Royal*, still denied her refit, had staged a demonstration of how difficult it is to hit a moving ship without having lots of aircraft available. When the battleship *Strasbourg* broke out to sea under escort of half a dozen destroyers six of the carrier's Swordfishes spotted her, cruising at 28 knots and unhurt by the bombs previously dropped. They flew up and down 100 feet above the sea, waiting like cats for the moment to pounce. As soon as the sun had set behind the great ship they went into the attack, flying low against the loom of the land. Inexperienced in such matters, as was everybody else in July, 1940, the pilots had no reason to believe it possible that they could penetrate the destroyer screen. The French anti-aircraft gunners had given ample proof of competence. The upshot of it was that only one torpedo hit its target and it seemed to do little enough damage.

More experience was gained next day. *Strasbourg*'s sister *Dunkerque* – of all names in that month – was shown by spotters to be grounded in Oran harbour but probably still operational. Two squadrons of *Ark Royal*'s Swordfish were told to finish her off. This time they went in at sunrise rather than sunset. Six Swordfishes, in line ahead, swooped down in a shallow dive from 7,000 feet almost to sea level, over the breakwater and straight at the ship from out of the sun. Four out of six torpedoes found their target and there was little opposition. The second and third waves were far more roughly handled but no aircraft was lost.

The experience was soon absorbed by all who had to do with such matters. Aircraft could engage moving ships with torpedoes, though it was by no means an easy thing to do. They could certainly smash up a ship in harbour more effectively than could battleships with 15" guns, provided only that surprise could be achieved. Most importantly, for this was quite unknown territory, it was now discovered that torpedo-carrying aircraft were able to ply their trade at night. This could make all the difference in an age where such refinements as radar were almost unknown.

On 10 June, 1940, Italy declared war on Great Britain and on the following day the Regia Aeronautica delivered the first of its many raids on Malta. The choice of moment for the throwing down of Mussolini's gauntlet may not have been exactly noble, but it was more respectable than the behaviour of his Japanese allies when their time came. Pound and Cunningham differed in their views on the survivability of *Glorious* once this had happened, but they had been agreed that she should be used in a last fling at Taranto before the end came. *Glorious*, however, was gone, leaving no heir. For the time being the Mediterranean fleet would simply have to take whatever punishment was coming, intercept Italian convoys to Libya by every possible means, and hope for better times.

It did now at least look like a fleet, with the old Jutland battleships back in the line and their near-contemporary *Eagle* ready and willing to do what she could in proclaiming the arrival of a new age. As she had only just arrived from the China station, along with a dozen submarines, it was hardly to be expected that ship and aircrews would be at concert pitch. *Eagle*, however, had not been born as *Almirante Cochrane* for nothing and her feats were soon to equal those of Cochrane's *Speedy* back in Nelson's time. Though nothing much to look at, practically unarmed, unarmoured and in need of continual minding *Eagle* carried seventeen Swordfishes and some of the best pilots and observers going. They were soon at work. The Admiral, though not unappreciative, was not satisfied. He had been promised the fine brand new *Illustrious* and it was her that he wanted above all things.

The melancholy business of the French fleet at Mers-el-Kebir on 3 July came and went. Admiral Cunningham, now much reinforced in Alexandria and flying his flag once again from a battleship, his old *Warspite*, made the best terms he could with his neighbour there, the French Admiral Godefroy. The Royal Navy is always courteous almost to a fault. There were strong grounds for suspecting the French ships in Alexandria of keeping up a steady stream of reports that would have found their way to Rome. After all, the cardinal principles of the French Navy have always been 'Fear God: hate the English'. They had no cause for complaint over their treatment there. No attempt was made to stop their knavish tricks.

Admiral Riccardi, Chief of the Italian Naval Staff, had at his disposal ships equal in numbers and better in quality than anything that the Mediterranean Fleet could bring against him. His two new battleships alone could have given him dominance; added to his Cavours and a land-based air force of quality he had the power to make the Mediterranean into *'Mare Nostrum'* indeed.

Against him was a force of battleships beautiful to look at but, for the most part, useless. *Malaya*, on Cunningham's own testimony, was not to be relied on because of 'condenseritis'. The boilers in *Royal Sovereign* and *Ramillies* were dying. The latter ship had been a liability from birth. When launched at Beardmores yard on the Clyde in 1917 she had charged across the river, hit the opposite bank, cracked her stern post, damaged her bottom and destroyed the larger of her two rudders. Because no dock on the Clyde was big enough to repair her, *Ramillies* had to be towed to Liverpool under heavy escort. On the way she ran aground again and did herself even more damage. *Ramillies* was always regarded as doubtful value in battle. Fortunately she did not often have to figure in one.

In Cunningham's fleet only the elaborately rebuilt *Warspite* carried guns that would match the 15-inches of the Littorios; even that was not a certainty. Most of his cruisers were in much the same case, small, old and perilously near to being completely worn out. When to that was added a general shortage of ammunition and luxuriant growths of Alexandria's famous weed on all bottoms, it becomes plain that the Mediterranean Fleet was nothing like as dangerous as it looked. If the expression 'paper tiger' had been in use late in 1940 it could aptly have been applied.

Admirals Riccardi and Cunningham had met socially before the war and the Italian had admitted to a proper reverence for the Immortal Memory. So much so, he had assured his guest, that he kept a copy of the life of Nelson (he did not say which one) on his cabin table and dipped into it regularly. It could have been rather less serviceable to him than would have been the memoirs of Quintus Fabius Maximus, Cunctator, for no Italian Admiral would ever seek a fleet action. There was no need for it. His submarines and bountiful aircraft could do the business of battleships better and less expensively. The talents of his best officers took other shapes.

Successors to Luigi Rizzo and Major Rosetti were doubtless to be found – as they were – and there were the useful mines. By judicious mine-laying off Alexandria – something the Italian submarines tried to do, though not very hard even though Cunningham was known to have no sweepers – he might have interned practically the whole of the Mediterranean Fleet, save only for such sea-gypsies as might be outside. That achieved, the Regia Aeronautica could take over. The excellent Savoia-Marchetti 79, well practised during the Spanish war against unarmed freighters commanded by the likes of the famous 'Potato' Jones, carried a bomb load of more than a ton and could operate from a ceiling at which no gun could bother it. The Fiat BR 20 had a load half as big again; the CANT Z5066 seaplane, looking like a Schneider Trophy competitor with a torpedo between its floats, recalled Captain Guidoni; the same firm's flying boat, the Z501, had a range of more than 600 miles. There was no shortage of any of them and bases were conveniently close by in both Libya and the Dodecanese. It would not have been too difficult, or so it appeared, to bomb Alexandria into uselessness.

The Italian bombers, however, concentrated more in attacking ships at sea. *Warspite*, their most dangerous enemy, was bombed thirty-four times in one day; somebody on board claimed to have counted 400 of them coming down. The other ships were not neglected. *Eagle* counted nearly as many, and *Eagle* was not armoured. Sir Andrew Cunningham, writing after the war, asserted that, 'It is not too much to say of those early months that the Italians' high-level bombing was the best I have ever seen, far better than the German'. Mark well the words 'early months' and 'high-level'. The cause would alter before very long. Until then the Regia Aeronautica bombed Alexandria regularly and with surprisingly little effect. The Fleet remained in being and a small airfield was created at Dekheila, some 8 miles west of the City, in order to provide some sort of base for whichever of the few Fleet Air Arm squadrons might want to use it.

It is not, nor ever has it been, the habit of the Royal Navy to wait for the King's enemies to hit first. Throughout June the Fleet had been carrying out coat-trailing exercises off the Italian coast, mutely inviting Riccardi to come out and fight. He had better sense. Malta was being harassed, British submarines were disappearing at an alarming rate – probably through mines – and the Regia Aeronautica was not doing all that badly. Given its numbers and the quality of its aircraft it would probably do better still as it gained experience. There was no point in risking his fine ships to no good purpose. Should any of them meet with misfortune then the coastal towns of Italy might well come under the guns.

There were better methods open to those who really understood sea warfare of a Mediterranean kind. The Italian fleet, with resident seaplanes to keep it informed about everything its enemy was doing, could cruise about at ease; whenever it needed anything, from routine maintenance to major repairs, there were some of the best naval bases in the world just under its lee. The British could sneer as much as they pleased about pusillanimity but all they could do was to wear themselves out to no great end.

Perhaps, when they had ground their ships down sufficiently, Admiral Riccardi might order offensive action. It could very well be combined with something done by the land forces. General Graziani in Libya had an army bigger by far than that of

General Wavell and infinitely better equipped. He did not seem to be doing anything much with it for the time being. The navies could ambush each other's convoys and wait upon events.

The nearest thing to a Mediterranean Jutland came on 9 July, 1940, almost entirely by accident. A strong Italian fleet returned from the direction of Libya to which it had just taken a convoy. Admiral Cunningham, similarly employed, was not far off. In accordance with the custom of the sea neither was aware of the other's presence until a Swordfish of 815 Squadron brought the news of an enemy being in sight. There followed one of the last of the old-style sea fights, a proper sailors' affair with hardly any interference from the air branch. A salvo from *Warspite*'s guns, cocked up at an almost impossible angle, scored a fair hit on the Cavour-class battleship *Cesare*. *Eagle* contributed everything that a small and obsolescent carrier could do. Possibly more. One of her Swordfish scored a hit on a cruiser, though it did not seem to do her much harm. The Italian fleet, much occupied in chasing five British light cruisers whose plight looked hopeless, decided that enough was enough. The fine ships first made smoke and then made for home. A Swordfish from *Eagle* sank one of the Italian destroyers at anchor at Augusta on the following day.

Though there was no denying that Cunningham's men had all the moral ascendancy of a tom-cat over a spaniel the fact remained that the Italian fleet, even without *Cesare*, was still the more powerful by far. It had, however, nothing as useful for many purposes as HMS *Eagle*. Three days later, as part of the convoy escort, the old carrier arrived in Malta with three Gladiators to thicken up the flimsy air defences of the island. As *Eagle* could not accommodate fixed-wing machines in her hangar they had to be carried on the flight deck. *Eagle* had no fighter pilots; her aircrews were all TSR, but it happened that the Commander (Flying), Keighly-Peach, had once been trained in that mystery. Since they arrived in the middle of the usual air-raid the Commander (Flying) and two volunteer pilots took the Gladiators into the air and shot down 'a shadower and two or three bombers'. Admiral Cochrane would have mightily approved. That done, *Eagle* returned to the Levant, raided Tobruk twice, bagging a tanker, two destroyers and a couple of merchant ships.

'K-P', who died in March, 1995, at the age of 92, encountered

the distaste for 'air' held by some senior officers well before the war. When he joined the then Rear-Admiral Cunningham in 1935 he was asked, 'Do you intend to keep that thing on your sleeve whilst on my staff?' 'That thing' being his 'wings', Keighly-Peach replied that he did. And was grudgingly allowed to.
(*Daily Telegraph*, 8 March, 1995.)

824 Squadron, *Eagle*'s Swordfish crews, had one outstanding success during the last days in which she alone represented the Navy's air power. On the strength of a report from Special Intelligence, some Blenheims of the RAF (the new Glenn L. Martin Marylands had not yet arrived) closely examined the doings of some Italian warships in the Gulf of Bomba, west of Tobruk. It soon became clear that they were up to no good and needed liquidation. A flight of three Swordfishes, led by Captain Patch of the Royal Marines – adding a new dimension to the motto of his Corps – moved to the airfield of Sidi Barrani; at dawn on 22 August they took off, loaded with torpedoes, made a 50-mile circuit in order to arrive from the least expected quarter and set about their work. With three torpedoes between them they accounted for two submarines, a destroyer and the depot ship *Monte Gargano*. Not merely a good bag, but more than at first it appeared. The submarine *Iride* was carrying a party of Italian frogmen, the true descendents of Rossetti and Paolucci, who meditated mischief among the capital ships snugly moored in Alexandria. Though few people would have remembered it outside Italy, the battleship had enemies other than bigger battleships, submarines, aircraft and the ordinary perils of the deep. Even as the most accomplished of swordsmen is at the mercy of any 3rd Class shot with a revolver, so were the most powerful of ships frighteningly vulnerable even at the time of what seemed their greatest safety. Patch and his companions well earned the decorations that came their way.

Soon after this valuable feat *Eagle* had to accept that she had become the junior partner, for, as part of the convoy curiously called 'Hats', *Illustrious*, with her squadron of Fulmar fighters as well as more Swordfishes, came to Alexandria. Along with her came the battleship *Valiant* which, though of little value for much else, also carried the new-fangled radar. *Illustrious* wasted no time. As Admiral Tovey – 'Old Splash Guts' the sailors called him – brought his squadron in from the north, it was duly escorted by an Italian spotter aircraft; Fulmars promptly shot it and its half-section down. This brought loud cheers from ships' companies who were becoming a little weary of being incessantly bombed without the ability to hit back.

For the next couple of months matters proceeded much as before, or so it seemed, but planning was going on. Anthony Eden, Secretary of State for War, was in Cairo; so were Wavell, Longmore and Cunningham. Eden was back in London on 8 November, 'bringing tidings of a deadly secret but extremely welcome character', as Ismay* put it. The secret, disclosed only to the Prime Minister, the Defence Committee, the Service Ministers and their Chiefs of Staff, was that Wavell (to whom 'Hats' had just brought some badly-needed tanks) had decided not to await Graziani's attack but to take the offensive himself, and that at an early date. This intelligence naturally delighted everybody. Churchill, according to Ismay, 'purred like six cats'. That was putting it mildly. He was rapturously happy. 'At long last we are going to throw off the intolerable shackles of the defensive,' he declaimed. 'Wars are won by superior will-power. Now we will wrest the initiative from the enemy and impose our will upon him.' The Navy was more than willing to do its share, especially the Commander-in-Chief, Mediterranean, who had never held any other view.

They were put into words at the bar in the Cecil Hotel in Alexandria by the senior pilot of 819 Squadron, Michael Torrens-Spence. 'I am afraid Cunningham will have to do a Nelson,' he said. It was almost exactly what old 'Jackie' Fisher had said years before when he urged that the Kaiser's High Seas Fleet be 'Copenhagened'. The audience knew perfectly well what was meant. Nelson had done it with ships; Cunningham might have to try and achieve the same result by means more suited to the new generation. And this time it would not be another Copenhagen. Sir Andrew was not proposing to cut out a hostile fleet under the noses of its proprietor. It was going to be a slightly earlier Nelson he might take for his example.

Just 15 miles from Alexandria was Aboukir Bay, where Nelson

---

* General Sir Hastings Ismay, Chief of Staff to the Minister of Defence.

had once sailed his ships inshore of a fleet at anchor and smashed it where it lay. The Italian fleet was in much the same position as that of Admiral Brueys in 1798. To a British admiral who had learnt his history in *Britannia* the parallel would have been obvious. Sir Andrew had a strong sense of the Navy eternal, his most quoted aphorism being to the effect that a ship can be built in three years but it needs 300 to make a tradition. With the Immortal Memory beckoning, there was only one possible course open to him.

5

APPRECIATING THE SITUATION

When planning an operation it is always well to know the measure of one's enemy. Admiral Cunningham knew the Italians, and particularly their Navy, better than did most men. As he himself put it in his Memoirs, 'I have often reflected how curiously history repeats itself. When I left the Mediterranean as a young Commander in 1917 I knew it very well. Malta, the Adriatic, Greece, Crete, and a multitude of lovely islands in the Aegean were old friends. I served in the Mediterranean again between the wars.' This, indeed, was something of an understatement.

In 1938 Vice-Admiral Cunningham, second-in-command to Sir Dudley Pound, then Commander-in-Chief of the Fleet there, received a goodwill visit from an Italian squadron. Four battleships, led by *Conte di Cavour* and *Giulio Cesare*, had steamed into the Grand Harbour at Valletta, suitably escorted, and with, Cunningham guessed, the whole catering staff and band from one of the best hotels in Rome, pressed for the occasion. The ships were impressive. *Cavour* had been built at Spezia in 1911, *Cesare* at Genoa in the same year, in order to serve against the Turks during the invasion of Libya. Both had undergone substantial reconstruction between 1933 and 1937 and they now displaced something like 24,000 tons each. Their armour had been much strengthened over magazines, machinery and boiler spaces with belts amidships of just under 10 inches. Each of them carried two catapulted aircraft. A pair of sister ships, *Caio Diulio* and *Andrea Doria*, were still in the hands of re-builders who were making them more than a match for anything the Royal Navy could bring against them, save only the recently modernized *Warspite*. Taranto had not been a lucky place for the Cavours. A fifth ship of the class, *Leonardo da Vinci*, had blown up there on 2 August, 1912.

Not on display were the newest battleships of all. *Littorio* and *Vittorio Veneto*, both of 35,000 tons and with nine 15-inch guns apiece, had been delivered in the summer of 1937. Two more, *Roma* and *Impero*, were due to join the Fleet in the early summer of 1940, which they did, just before Italy came into the war. A lot of care had gone into the designing of the battleships and of the heavy 8-inch-gunned cruisers of the Zara and Bolzano classes. Nobody failed to notice how generously they were all equipped with AA weapons. The Cavours mounted either eight or ten guns roughly to the British 3.7" and something like forty machine guns of varying sizes. The Fiat-Revelli medium machine gun and the heavier Breda, though not as good as the Oerlikon, were still better than their equivalents in the British service.

From the opulence of *Hood*'s Admiral's cabin, ward room and deck canopied for dancing, Cunningham was able to take stock of the kind of enemy he might some day have to fight. The senior officers, some of them almost certainly old associates of the Kaiser's war, were staunch royalists and carried themselves like the gentlemen they were. The younger men seemed to be of a different mettle; probably brave and competent enough but boorish in their behaviour as guests on or around the dance floor. Very possibly they found it expedient not to fall out with the political commissars, or whatever the fascists called them – curious figures attached to most ships in the implausible character of 'springers' – PT instructors. The Admiral bade farewell to his guests with no great unease about the outcome of another kind of meeting.

When that came about it was not Cunningham's fleet in the Levant that got in the first blow. His old *Britannia* term and class-mate James Somerville, commanding the newly-formed Force H and based on Gibraltar, was the first to taste blood. Force H, which had had the lamentable duty of taking out the French fleet, was in fact *Ark Royal* with a very heavy escort.

In passing it may be worth mentioning the position of Spain. General Franco has never enjoyed a good press in this country, a state of affairs little short of ingratitude. Science had progressed since Eliott's Great Siege of 1783 and the harbour under the Rock could so easily have been rendered useless by a few heavy batteries on the Spanish mainland. Franco stood up to Hitler not because he was a friend to France or Britain – he had little enough reason to love either – but because he was a patriotic Spanish officer. Had he weakened and allowed the Germans free passage across his starving country the Mediterranean must almost certainly have been lost to us. Through his non-hostility Force H, if not actually master of the Western Mediterranean, certainly ensured the survival of Malta and the passage of the most necessary convoys to about the half-way mark. There Cunningham's ships took over, along with their aircraft. In the beginning Force H mustered not merely *Ark Royal* as the source of her air power; the veteran *Argus*, older than most of those who sailed in her, took to Malta in July, 1940, the dozen Hurricanes that kept the island's head above water.

The first bombs to fall upon Italian soil came from a squadron of *Ark Royal*'s Swordfish early in the morning of 2 August, 1940. Three more of them busied themselves with laying mines. The object was to beat up the base at Cagliari, on the southern tip of Sardinia, and to gain practical experience at no excessive cost. It was needed. The fifth Swordfish in the deck park veered to starboard during take-off, hit a pompom and fell into the sea, drowning all its crew. The remainder, having begun by losing their way, managed to achieve all that they had set out to do. In the space of about a minute and lashed by machine-gun fire the Swordfishes dropped their mines and dived in with their bombs. Buildings were set on fire, four aircraft on the water were hit and a single Swordfish was brought down without the crew being hurt. The Regia Aeronautica kept its distance.

There were lessons and they were learned. A round trip of 150 miles was just within the limits of a Swordfish's fuel tank, but only just. Navigation amongst mountains needed special study. *Ark Royal* hit Elmas again in September, as part of the elaborate operation to get the 'Hats' convoy through but this time with less success. Mist and low cloud made target identification very difficult indeed. With that over *Ark Royal* was packed off to take a hand in the grotesque Dakar business.

With the arrival of *Illustrious* as part of the 'Hats' convoy it became the turn of Admiral Cunningham's end of the Mediterranean. The main Italian bases were Genoa, Spezia, Livorno and Taranto and it was in these that the battle fleet harboured up. The nearest and best known of them should be vulnerable to carrier-borne aircraft given the long-range tanks that *Illustrious* had brought with her.

Thus it was that the eternity of the Navy proclaimed itself once again. Three old *Britannias*, Admiral Cunningham, Rear-Admiral Lyster and Air Marshal Longmore, took counsel together and plotted out a battle of the future, a battle that would shape the course of sea warfare for a long time to come. Since their education had been what it was they would all have been familiar with the Book of Common Prayer and in particular with the 'Prayer to be said before a Fight at Sea against any Enemy'. The middle part runs, 'Thou sittest in the throne judging right, and therefore we make our address to thy Divine Majesty in this our necessity, that thou wouldest take the cause into thine own hand and judge between us and our enemies'. Whether or not there was any connection between the old Prayer and the planned attack on an enemy fleet it is no longer possible to ascertain. Only the fact remains that the raid on Taranto by the Fleet Air Arm was given the name 'Operation Judgment'. At least it sounds apter than 'Hats'.

All these senior officers, with a vastness of combined experience hard to equal, reckoned that the thing could, and should, be done. It was for Lyster to report and advise the First Sea Lord, which he did. The reply was an unenthusiastic consent, explaining that 'Only sailors who live in ships should attack other ships'. It was enough. Sir Andrew Cunningham who, in his youth, had fought against the Boers under that almost legendary post-Captain 'Prothero The Bad', approved. And all the necessary preliminaries were put in hand.

6

DRAMATIS PERSONAE

Lyster's plan of 1935 would serve for a first draft but since then
the cause had altered. The modified version, proposed by
Admiral Pound in 1938, when the Swordfish had entered the lists,
looked more promising, but now that a second carrier, bigger by
far than *Glorious* had been, would operate alongside *Eagle* something drastic might well be done. *Illustrious* was a new ship but a
few of her pilots and observers had learned their business in
Glorious; *Eagle*'s young men had already given their proofs in the
Mediterranean. From Alexandria to Taranto in a straight line is
something like 800 miles. The carriers would have to be brought
to a point about 40 miles to the west of Cephalonia before releasing their hawks. The obvious need to make sure that the Fleet
would not be steaming into an ambush would have to be dealt
with by the RAF from Malta. Now that the new and fast Glenn
Martin Marylands had arrived this ought not to present too much
difficulty. Nor would this be their only task. An attack on a well
established and properly defended naval base was not something
to be lightly undertaken, especially by aircraft as vulnerable as the
lumbering Swordfish.

Like every other operation of war, this one demanded that a
choice be made between several difficulties. Eliminating the fighting power of the Italian fleet in Taranto harbour must be
something for which a price would have to be paid. Even were
every ship flying Italian colours to be sent to the bottom there
would still be other ships in other harbours, none of them all that
far away. On the other hand the loss of many Swordfishes and
their experienced crews would be catastrophic; the few remaining

Torpedo-Strike-Reconnaissance machines left would be woefully insufficient for their duties, and Fulmars, fighters and nothing else, could not do Swordfish work. The word 'kamikaze' would not come into the language for quite a long time but the idea was not new. The Swordfishes must not be thrown into battle unless they were given a decent chance of surviving it. The raid would have to take place at night, a circumstance that demanded all help from the moon and flares dropped by the attackers. They had proved superfluous in the second raid on Cagliari since the Italians had themselves illuminated the place with anti-aircraft weapons known as 'flaming onions', but there was no reason to suppose that they would oblige a second time. The risk of Italian night-fighters being alerted and arriving on the scene in time to chase after the intruders could be ignored; it was known that they had no such aircraft available.

Then it was necessary to calculate the weight and type of projectile to be employed. Recent photographs taken by the RAF had shown plainly that the battleships were wearing their torpedo nets and that the anchorage was well supplied with barrage balloons.

Net and balloon were both reckoned to be of the highest importance in the defence of motionless ships. Much thought had been given to the shielding of those in the Mar Grande of Taranto and it was not the fault of the Italian engineers concerned that they were something less than perfect. Barrage balloons were a mild joke to Londoners, but London was not troubled by dive bombers. The business of the balloon was to force intruders to stay at a respectful height on pain of being caught up in a forest of steel cables. To a pilot obliged to plunge through them they were anything but amusing. In harbour they naturally worked in tandem with the underwater nets.

It had been calculated that the big ships in Taranto needed 12,800 metres of netting in order that they might be properly cocooned. By November, 1940, only 4,200 had been laid and a further 2,900 were still in store. Italy had several defended bases and a monthly output of 3,600 metres was not enough for the needs of them all. The netting available had been put down in the way best fitted to limit the torpedo-launching points available either to aircraft or to any possible successors to Luigi Rizzo. Three sides of a square in the north-east quadrant of the Mar

Grande, the open quarter being close to the entrance to the inner harbour, gave shelter to the heavy cruisers *Fiume, Zara* and *Gorizia*. Between the easternmost side of the line of nets and shoreline was Italy's Battleship Row, with *Duilio, Cesare, Littorio, Vittorio Veneto* and *Andrea Doria* all safely anchored and in that order from north to south.

The balloons were in worse case than the nets. Recent storms had damaged or destroyed many of them and the local production of hydrogen gas had not been able to keep up supplies. The twenty-seven that were in service on the night of the attack were divided into three sections. The first, on the west side, were moored alongside the seaward line of nets covering the cruisers*; the second, outside the breakwater called Diga di Tarantola, ended at its north point where a short length of net joined the tip of the Diga to the netted area. The last eleven balloons were on land, along the south-eastern shore of the Mar Grande and covering the Floating Dock and the Oil Storage Depot. Given the equipment available to them and the knowledge that no strike had ever been attempted by aircraft on a defended port it is hard to see how the Italians could have managed things better in order to keep their ships safe from attack by torpedo.

The only ones available to the Fleet in late 1940 were, in any event, a little behind the times. The 18-inch Mk XIIs† were to be set to run at 27 knots with a depth of 33 feet – sufficient to circumvent any net – and with 100 yards run off the safety range. All would be set to remain alive at the end of their run and each contained a roll of cable which unwound and held the angle after dropping as well as inhibiting 'porpoising' or diving too deeply. Only contact with the water was needed in order to set the propellors turning and to speed the missile on its way. The Japanese 24-inch, oxygen-powered Long Lance was a more powerful weapon in every way but its time had not yet come. First War

* This line of balloons is not mentioned in the extracts from the report of the Italian Commander-in-Chief Afloat to his Chief of Naval Staff but is shown on the Admiralty's Plan 7.

† Lieutenant-Commander Wellham, whose acquaintance any possible reader will soon be making, has been kind enough to tell me that the reference in the Official Report to a Mk XIII is probably a misprint. There never was a Mk XIII.

pattern torpedoes such as the Mk XII ought to be good enough to sink First War battleships such as the Cavours. What they could achieve against newer ships like *Littorio* and *Vittorio Veneto* remained to be seen.

All were equipped with the Duplex pistol, a British invention that was hoped to improve performance substantially. The Taranto crews had a personal interest, for Captain Boyd of *Illustrious*, when in command of HMS *Vernon*, had had much to do with its invention. The Duplex had at its heart a coil with thousands of turns of fine wire mounted on a rod of Muntz metal. The current developed in the coil as the torpedo passed underneath a ship would fire the warhead even if there had been no actual contact. Great things were expected of the Duplex, and not without reason. The bombs promised little, for semi-armour-piercing affairs of 250-lbs apiece would be unlikely to cause serious damage to a heavily armoured ship, unless they were dropped squarely on it and in a vulnerable spot. For that reason the bombers were given the task of attending to the smaller and thinner-plated craft berthed in the Mar Piccolo as well as the old seaplane base and the oil storage depot. The flares, made by the firm of Brock, were known from long experience to be utterly reliable.

Admiral Cunningham, like all naval officers, had a proper sense of history; the season of the year being what it was and the moon being where it was wanted, he decided to mount his attack on 21 October. It is not necessary to insult the reader by explaining its significance. Admiral Riccardi would have known well enough. The aircrews, at concert pitch, were ready to go but a serious fire in *Illustrious'* hangar put paid to any anniversary celebration. When it was suggested that the end of the same month might serve there were unanswerable objections. In the first place night attacks, never before attempted in earnest, demanded long and painstaking attention to detail and the pilots still needed more rehearsal time. And, in any event, there would be no moon.

One may fairly guess that Rear Admiral Lyster was not allowing himself to be rushed into launching his strike until he was in all respects ready; the moon had a very definite place in his plans. It had to be in a carefully selected position, high and still in the east at the time of arrival in order that his torpedo-carriers approaching from the west would find the Italian battleships illuminated fairly well by the light of Nature. Only from that point of the compass could decent targets be presented without the need for aircraft to make a dangerous overland run-in so as to circumvent the nets.

His aircrews were occupying themselves at every possible moment with perfecting the dropping of bombs or torpedoes by night, but the strike at Taranto was decreed by Their Lordships to be only a part of a larger operation. The Italian invasion of Greece had proved not to be the walk-over that Mussolini had expected. To the surprise of everybody, the Greeks were putting up a fairly stout resistance and they deserved all the help that could be given. In addition to Greece and Crete – the Navy looked longingly at the Suda Bay anchorage – Malta was in straits and needed relief even more than did the newest ally. This meant convoys, and convoys meant Somerville's Force 'H' coming in from one end of the Mediterranean to a point 165 miles West of Sicily; once there they were in Sir Andrew Cunningham's parish and responsibility for keeping the Regia Aeronautica at arm's length fell to *Illustrious* and *Eagle* as reliefs to *Ark Royal* and *Argus*.

A fast convoy was coming from Malta to Alexandria. Once that was safely on the move, the rest of the Navy's plan could be put into force, not merely an air strike on the ships in Taranto harbour but also a cruiser raid on Italian shipping in the Straits of Otranto. The whole affair was given the operational title of MB8. To achieve its aims Sir Andrew divided his fleet into three task groups, a new expression but a durable one. Lyster and his carriers would hit Taranto, Vice-Admiral Pridham-Wippell would take his cruisers and destroyers to seek out and destroy whatever Italian convoys they might find and the Admiral would keep the remainder under his own hand as a general reserve. The cruisers had a small action at almost exactly the same time as that of the carriers, sinking four merchant ships and damaging a torpedo-boat without receiving a hit. Nevertheless, it was the carriers that held the heavy end of the stick.

Bad luck seemed to dog them from the start. The final plan, given out on 28 October, still had parts for *Eagle* and her crews, but *Eagle* was in poor shape. The old ship had been much knocked about by near-misses from Italian bombs and her aviation petrol supply was giving trouble. There was nothing for it but to leave

8. Sub-Lieutenant (A) Ronald Bailey, DSC, RN

11. Lieutenant E.W. Clifford DSC, RN

9. Sub-Lieutenant (A) J. Buscall, RNVR

12. Sub-Lieutenant P.D. Jones DSC, RN

10. Lieutenant G.A. Carline, DSC, RN

13. Lieutenant H.R.B. Janvrin, DSC, RN

14. Lieutenant (A) L.J. Kiggell, DSC, RN

15. Lieutenant C.B. Lamb, DSO, DSC, RN

16. Sub-Lieutenant (A) A.F.X. Mardel-Ferreira, RNVR

17. Sub-Lieutenant (A) J.W. Neale, DSC, RN

18. Captain Oliver Patch, DSC, RM; the only Royal Marine officer to take part in the attack on Taranto.

19. Sub-Lieutenant (A) W.C. Sarra, RN

20. Lieutenant N.J. Scarlett, DSC, RN

23. Lieutenant F.M.A. Torrens-Spence, DSC, RN

21. Lieutenant H.J. Slaughter, RN

24. Lieutenant (A) J.W.G. Welham, DSC, RN

22. Lieutenant H.A. Swayne, RN

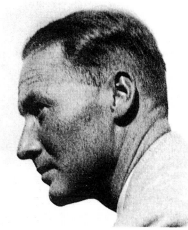

25. Lieutenant-Commander K. Williamson, DSO, RN

26. Sub-Lieutenant A.L.O. Wray, DSC, RNVR

27. Captain Denis Boyd, Captain of HMS *Illustrious* at the time of the Taranto raid.

28. Captain Ian Robertson RN, Commander Flying HMS *Illustrious* at the time of the Taranto raid.

her at Alexandria, after having transferred five Swordfishes and eight crew members to the bigger vessel. *Illustrious* herself was not exempt from difficulties. During the convoy phase, between 6 November when she sailed and the 11th when the action took place, three of her Swordfishes had been ditched in the sea by reason of water contamination of their fuel from an oil tanker. Some hasty rearrangements had to be made but by 20.40 hours on Armistice Day, 1940, *Illustrious* and her escort had reached the springboard point, some 40 miles to the west of Kabbo Point on the island of Cephalonia.*

The hangar fire in *Illustrious* had taken out several aircraft, some of them permanently. Deducting also the three with contaminated fuel, the total available for the strike came down to twenty-one. They were drawn unequally, for it could not be helped, from 813, 815, 819 and 824 Squadrons, FAA. The crews were reduced to pilot and observer alone in order to make room for the long-range petrol tank which was carried by the torpedo craft in the rear cockpit. The conversion of the Swordfish into a flying machine crammed with every kind of explosive and combustible commodity hardly made the affair less risky, but there was nothing for it. The rear Lewis gun was never highly regarded and its absence bothered nobody; more important was the fact that once a machine had passed out of sight it would be lost to the world with no sort of radio contact.

The attack was planned to be delivered in two stages with an hour between them. The first flight, having the probable advantage of surprise, would be the stronger. It would be made up of ten Swordfishes from *Illustrious* plus another two from *Eagle*. Six would carry torpedoes, these being the Heavy Brigade of the assault. Two would carry four each of the 250-lb bombs, in addition to the sixteen parachute flares that were their main equipment. The remaining four, the bombers pure and simple, were loaded with six bombs apiece. In addition each aircraft carried, as a matter of course, a couple of flares to be used as occasion might demand.

All the crews had been carefully briefed but it would have been out of the question to have been over-specific. Since the torpedo-

---

* To be precise, 38° 12' N, 19° 47' E.

carriers would be diving into heavy fire over a fairly small area the only order possible was given. The torpedomen, the decisive arm of the operation, were to go for the battleships. It mattered not which battleship each pilot might select; at such close quarters there was every chance that a torpedo missing one might hit another, especially with the benefits of the Duplex pistol. The bombers were given as their primary target the line of cruisers and destroyers in the Mar Piccolo. Here there would be no need to pick and choose; the second target for bombs would be the seaplane base, home to the irritating Italian flying boats that watched every movement of every ship in the Mediterranean Fleet, or so it seemed. The flare-droppers alone were given exact orders. Their chosen lines were oblique to and south-eastward of the moored battleships in order to help the moon in making silhouettes of them for the benefit of attackers coming in across the Mar Grande. That done, they were to use their bombs on the oil installations; not that these were of much importance but the aircraft were already near them and might add a little to the confusion. Bombers and flare-droppers alike would, it was hoped, do something to divert the Italian gunners from the more dangerous torpedo planes.

The briefing gave the positions of the battleships, balloons, nets and gun-sites. With that information supplied, it was left to the pilots and their leaders to settle the directions of approach. They were all men selected because they had had experience of making torpedo attacks on harbours as part of their training and knew pretty well what they were in for. This was not going to be like the attack on a moving ship for which a co-ordinated scheme was needed. Instead it would call for a plan agreed between the players followed by unusual virtuosity on the part of each officer at the controls. At that point in the war it is unlikely that the qualities needed would be found anywhere else.

After discussion it was agreed that the first sub-flight of torpedo-carriers should, like so many young Lochinvars, come in from the west, cross the triangular island of San Pietro, with its AA batteries at each corner, at 4,000 feet and then dive straight at the battleships. Once the torpedoes had gone they would turn smartly about and fly home. The second wave would fly a course further north, crossing the submerged breakwater beyond San

Pietro, above the Mar Grande and the moored cruisers and, after a swing to the south, down into torpedo-dropping range of their big targets. This should keep them from diving into the barrage balloons and, with luck, they ought to be able to release their missiles inside the nets. The bombers and flare droppers, under no necessity of coming down almost to sea level, could set their courses more or less directly with less risk of entanglement in the balloon cables. Visibility, upon which everything turned, ought not to be too bad with ¾ moon helping out from behind the main flare line.*

The second striking force, nine Swordfishes in all, would begin work 20 minutes after the first one had quitted the scene. If the first strike had had the good fortune to catch the Italians slightly off guard there was no hope at all of the second having such advantage. With only five torpedo planes available there were the same number of battleships waiting for them, to say nothing of the cruisers *Fiume*, *Zara* and *Gorizia*, all lying snugly inside the nets and handsomely equipped with AA guns.

The five pilots were well aware that their task was to get in among the battleships but it was out of the question to be specific about who went for which. To have laid it down that 'You go for *Littorio* while I set about *Vittorio Veneto*' would have been an obvious recipe for failure and probably for the loss of all five. This was a state of affairs demanding skill, virtuosity, and split-second decisions depending entirely upon what each pilot might see as affording him the most promising target. It was for this sort of thing that they had practised so long.

The bombers needed no such liberty of action. Their duties

---

* Not everybody approved the use of flares. As Lieutenant-Cdr Wellham put it in a letter to the author: 'The question is a very vexed one. My dislike in general is because of the effect on night vision when they go out and the fact that, when obliged to fly at a low height, such as in a torpedo attack, they tend to illuminate the aircraft and help the flak. On the other hand if the target and defences are on one side of the flares and one can attack from the other, dark, side it is possible to gain some surprise. . . . At Taranto it was like daylight with a clear sky, a brilliant moon and light from all the tracer. In that case we didn't need flares and, personally, I would rather not have had them.' But, as Lieutenant-Cdr Wellham says, 'If it is a dark night without moon they can be essential to identify the target (and) the moon can be obscured by cloud.' Not an easy decision to have to make.

were to be the same as those carried out by their opposite numbers in the first wave. The smaller ships in the Mar Piccolo along with the oil storage depot were to receive their attention, doing what damage a dozen bombs of middling size might do; the flare-droppers, having completed their main business, could chip in with four more.

The aircrews taking part in the attack were not, nor could they have been, an altogether homogeneous body, for a year and a quarter of war – very nearly – had brought about some changes. Even so, this must have been the first naval operation in history where no participant was below commissioned rank. One solitary midshipman represented all gunrooms. All the pilots, saving the one from the Royal Marines, were regular officers of the Royal Navy, trained by the Navy itself in the days before expansion had led to the great dispersion of places of instruction; Pensacola and Miami in the United States and, above all, Kingston in Canada would be the sources of new pilots, but not yet. Of the observers, seventeen were 'pukka RN', the remaining four coming from the Royal Naval Volunteer Reserve.*

Each of the Striking Forces was commanded – led would be a better word since no communication between aircraft, save for Aldis lamps, existed – by a Lieutenant-Commander RN of much experience. The first came under Lieutenant-Commander K. Williamson – 'Hooch' to his peers – who had joined the Service as far back as 1924, qualified as a pilot in 1929, and had been one of the first to join *Courageous* when she had been commissioned in the following year. He had been a squadron commander, of 822 Squadron, since 1938, and had recently joined *Illustrious* in the same capacity. His observer, Lieutenant N.J. Scarlett, one of the three sons of that Commander F.R. Scarlett who had been DAD Naval Staff in 1918, at 30 years of age, was only a little his junior. He had joined as Midshipman in 1928, served in a number of cruisers and smaller ships but had trained as an observer and taken to the air in 1937 with *Glorious*. Scarlett, commonly called

* Civilians called up under the Military Service Acts who opted for the sea service and were given officer training were not given temporary RN commissions but those of the RNVR. This could be misleading, for as time passed fewer and fewer of those wearing the wavy stripe were, strictly, either Volunteers or Reservists.

'Blood', was senior enough to say of his pilot that he had just come from the Admiralty and had never dropped a torpedo by night in his life. It was an unavoidable state of affairs, unless the entire business of naval aviation was to be turned over to very young men indeed. The tradition of brave, decorated, schoolboys from Gallipoli days was not to be repeated. Midshipman Bowker had been with *Hermes* in 1939 and with *Illustrious* since April, 1940.

Next in seniority to Williamson came Lieutenant Neil Kemp, RN, another old *Courageous* who had joined the Royal Navy as a Cadet in 1927 and, after the usual spell of duties undertaken by a sea officer between the wars, had taken to the air and qualified as a pilot six years later. He was a man highly regarded in the service. When he came to meet his death, not long after 'Judgment', a brother officer spoke of him as having had all the qualities to have made 'a wonderful Admiral'. In Swordfish L4K, of 815 Squadron, he had for observer Sub-Lieutenant R.A. Bailey, lately arrived on board *Illustrious* after having been observer to the Walrus amphibian carried by the cruiser HMS *York*.

Only a year behind Kemp in seniority came one of *Eagle*'s pilots, Lieutenant M.R. Maund, RN, who was also something of a veteran. He had served for eight years as watchkeeper in cruisers before qualifying as a pilot in 1936. Maund had been with 813 Squadron on board *Eagle* for the last couple of years; his observer Sub-Lieutenant W.A. Bull had been there for about half as long and they were accustomed to working together.

The next two pilots were Lieutenant Launcelot Kiggell – famous combination of names in an earlier war – and Charles Lamb. Kiggell was one of those who had come to the Fleet Air Arm by way of the RAF and had been with *Illustrious* for the past three years. Lamb had come by an even more circuitous path. He had begun his seafaring career as a Merchant Navy officer but had shared the experience of many such in finding employment hard to come by. It seemed sensible in the early 1930s to learn flying and to that end Lamb had joined the RAF. His wings were now five years old and in this war he had seen everything that had so far happened. From being the last man to land a Swordfish on the sinking *Courageous*, he had made twenty-nine sorties over Europe, doing everything from laying mines off Wilhelmshaven to dive-bombing German troops during the battle of France. His observer, Lieutenant K.C. Grieve also qualified for veteran status for he had spent no less than eleven years in battleships and cruisers before he took to flying in the vintage year of 1938. Kiggell's observer has been left until last, for Lieutenant H.R.B. Janvrin was unique among those who took part in this operation. Lamb calls him 'an easy-going 6-footer; nothing seemed to disturb his equanimity'. Cadet Janvrin of 1929 had been another of the sodality of 1938 observers; Vice-Admiral Sir Richard Janvrin hoisted his Flag in 1964, one of the few survivors of the carnage that lay just around the corner for so many of his mess-mates.

Williamson's sub-flight was completed by the two Swordfishes L4C and L4R. The former was flown by a pilot who, though in his early 20s, already wore the ribbon of the DSC. Julian Sparke, still only Sub-Lieutenant, had the reputation of being a thruster, a reputation that his short remaining life fully justified. He had been with *Illustrious* for the past year; his observer, Sub-Lieutenant J.W. Neale was another of the younger men and of about equal seniority to his pilot. Following L4C and in L4R were more of the young men, Sub-Lieutenants Douglas Macaulay RN and Sub-Lieutenant (A) A.L.O. Wray, RNVR. L4M was the machine of a more experienced hand, for Lieutenant Ian Swayne had three years as a Fleet Air Arm pilot behind him. His observer was a harbinger of things to come, for Sub-Lieutenant (A) J. Buscall, recently joined, was one of the new breed of RNVR officers commissioned from civil life soon after call-up.

Captain Patch, already with a DSO from Bomba Bay, as befitted the representative of the Royal Marines, was given more of a free hand; with Lieutenant D.G. Goodwin, RN, whose cadet-ship dated back more than fifteen years, Patch in E5A was sent to dive-bomb the cruisers in the Mar Piccolo. In his company, more or less, would be the least experienced crew of all, Sub-Lieutenant (A) W.C. Sarra, RN, and Mr Midshipman Bowker in L4L. They were to give their undivided attention to the wrecking of the sea-plane base. The last pair, aimed at the smaller ships in Mar Piccolo, were L4H, crewed by the young sub-lieutenants Forde and Mardel-Ferreira, and Eagle's E5Q carrying Lieut. (A) A.J.B. Murray and Sub.-Lieut (A) S.M. Paine.

The second strike, reduced to nine machines, would follow the same pattern with five torpedo-carriers and four with flares and bombs. The Heavy Brigade was to go for the battleships with torpedoes, while the flare-droppers and bombers were to repeat the work of their predecessors. The 250-lb semi-armour-piercing bomb had been used often enough before and nobody had serious doubts about its quality.

Lieutenant-Commander J.W. Hale, 'Ginger' to his peers, was the perfect choice as leader of the Second Striking Force. Like Williamson, he was a senior figure with already twenty years service behind him. Before assuming command of 819 Squadron he had served in turn in *Courageous* as long ago as 1931 and had commanded 825 Squadron – also Swordfish – in *Glorious* before the war. In intervals he had played Rugby both for the Navy and for England. Another pilot who, though not in Hale's present 819 Squadron, knew him well, described him as 'unshakeable as the Rock of Gibraltar'. His observer, Lieutenant G.A. Carline was another near-veteran, having joined the Navy in 1927 and enjoyed the usual 'salt horse' officer's appointments in everything from battleships to gunboats before taking to the air as an observer in 1938. He, too, was an Old *Courageous*, a well respected thing to be in 1940.

Hale's next astern in the torpedo attack would be E4H, crewed by two experienced RN officers, Lieutenant (A) G.W.L.A. Bayly and Lieutenant H.J. Slaughter. Bayly, having served his time as Midshipman, from 1932, had moved into the air and joined 824 Squadron in *Eagle* in February, 1938. His observer had only a little less sea service behind him before transferring to 813 Squadron, also aboard *Eagle*, in 1938. Both could, therefore, be reckoned experienced hands.

The remaining aircrews were, inevitably, an amalgam of youth and experience, the two being not mutually incompatible. The pilot of L5H, for example, combined both. Lieutenant Spencer (or 'Sprog') Lea had been apprentice to a sheep farmer in the Australian outback before feeling the call of the sea, 'and was a tough, sandy-haired warrior' with a gift of language that proclaimed his apprenticeship not to have been wasted. Sub-Lieutenant P.D. Jones, another regular, was observer. The next pilot, Lieutenant (A) J.W.G. Wellham of E5H, held the DSC for his part in the Bomba Bay affair and since leaving the RAF had served three years with the Navy. His observer, Pat

Humphreys, was also a man of distinction. By November, 1940, he had notched up fourteen years of service, from cadet in 1927 to observer in 1938, and had already been decorated with the Empire Gallantry Medal (later exchanged for the George Cross) for an act of bravery in Coronation year as a destroyer officer during the Spanish Civil War.*

Among the other crews were the Northern Irishman Michael Torrens-Spence, senior pilot in 819 Squadron and by common consent one of the Navy's very best fliers. He too was of the vintage that had worn midshipman's dirks in the early 1930s and had turned skywards when the Navy once more became master in its own house. Much the same could have been said of his observer 'Alfie' Sutton.

Slightly older was the pilot of L5B, Lieutenant R.W.V. Hamilton, who had served a decade of sea-time in battleships and cruisers before becoming another of the 1938 class of observers. After them came the junior men. Sub-Lieutenant (A) J.R.B. Weekes, Hamilton's companion on 11 November, was ten years behind him in seniority and had not been long in the ship.

Younger still were the crew of L4F, Lieutenant (A) R.G. Skelton, who had been in *Glorious* during 1938, and was the only RNVR officer in the second strike. Sub-Lieutenant (A) E.A. Perkins, 23 years old, had only been commissioned on 10 August and was new to the ship. One may without trying very hard imagine his pride at being the only non-regular officer to take part in so very important a show. He appears to have trained as observer while still a rating and to have achieved officer status only a short time before the battle. Two more months of life lay ahead of him. The crew of L5F, Lieutenants E.W. Clifford and G.R.M. Going, were both men of standing, having entered the service as midshipmen in 1932. Clifford had been the first to explore the new element with his pilot training dating back to 1935. Going, another of the 1938 class of observers, had interested himself in all aspects of the sea service; after serving in the new battleship *Nelson* he had explored the depths in the submarine *Starfish*. That done, he took to the air. Both these officers had joined 819 Squadron on board *Illustrious* earlier in 1940. The last pair,

* See Appendix II

Lieutenant (A) A.W.D. Morford and Sub-Lieutenant (A) R.A.F. Green, were both pre-war aircrew and, like so many of the others, had joined the Squadron and the ship only a few months before the action.

These were the gladiators, few enough in all conscience, who would take their obsolete aeroplanes and unreliable weapons through the defences of one of the world's great naval bases and wreak what damage they could on some of the most powerful warships afloat.

7

JUDGMENT DELIVERED

Taranto, an ancient town of something like 150,000 inhabi-
tants, had so far been troubled less by war than by foul
weather. During the first days of November heavy storms had
damaged or destroyed many of its protective ring of balloons and
it had not been possible to repair or replace them to anything near
the usual numbers. Such as were still serviceable, twenty-seven in
all, were kept permanently aloft at a uniform height of about
1,000 feet. The Mar Grande, anchorage for many merchant ships
in addition to its naval facilities, is roughly circular with a diam-
eter of something over 3 miles and carefully contrived means of
entrance.* The western, seaward, entrance is blocked at its middle
by the large island called San Pietro; from it extend submerged
breakwaters in both north-east and south-east directions; at the
extreme south-east of the harbour entrance, beyond the gap where
three AA gun batteries were moored, a mole named Diga di San
Vito connects with the mainland. Entry points for surface vessels
of all kinds were narrow and commanded by fire.

Around the circumference of the Mar Grande or mounted on
pontoons within it stood twenty-one batteries of 4-inch guns,
eighty-four heavy and 109 light machine guns and twenty-two
searchlights, 'mostly modern type, long range, placed on shore
and on pontoons', as the Italian Commander-in-Chief's report on
the defences puts it. These, of course, were merely the fixed
defences. The ships had guns and lights of their own, at least
doubling the volume of fire that could be turned on any visiting

* See Plan 7 on endpapers.

aircraft. The heavy cruisers mounted eighteen large-calibre machine guns apiece, the Cavour class battleships twice as many and the Littorios both carried a dozen medium-sized AA guns along with forty heavy automatics, all specifically designed and placed to take on enemy aircraft. On a cold calculation of probabilities it did not seem very likely that machines as slow and vulnerable as the Swordfish could hope to escape destruction when plunging into such a concentration of bullets and shells in so small a space. Nor was there any real hope, however pleasant it might be to imagine it, that the Italian Navy might be caught napping. The report mentioned before by the Italian Commander-in-Chief afloat, which fell into British hands later on, is quite clear about it: 'AA artillery. All in working order in accordance with plans which had been prepared for some time, with the addition of numerous machine guns recently arranged to deal with torpedo aircraft'. All ships were, so it said, in a state of complete readiness, with watchfulness at night and at dawn being intensified. 'Ships' main armaments were half-manned; AA guns fully so.' The orders to ships were clear enough: 'No barrage fire at the same time as that of shore batteries. Machine guns to be manned and fired with the main armament against aircraft visible to the naked eye or illuminated by searchlight.' The gunners were experienced and their weapons good.

Diving into this lethal goldfish bowl was going to be a desperately dangerous business and with nothing like certainty of success. All the same, the sudden eruption of noise as a dozen Pegasus engines roared into their dives could be expected to unsteady the strongest of nerves. It was the only factor to be counted upon apart from the skill and dexterity of the pilots. Knowing nearly all about this as they did, it was still a prospect regarded by the aircrews and their acolytes with the highest of spirits.

The Royal Navy was, so far, the only one to have used aircraft carriers in war and, though more than a year had passed, save in Norway, they had done nothing spectacular. Keeping roofs over convoys did not amount to anything exciting to people not concerned with seafaring matters. In addition, war with Italy was not the same as the fight to the death with Germany. It could almost have been said that Italy's war was of Italy's life a thing apart but it was Germany's whole existence. Young English gentlemen, as a matter of course, learnt Latin; few of them learned German. Italy, never an enemy since the Legions had left Britannia, posed no threat to the homeland. It was the purest coincidence that Mussolini, that same night, was planning to send his bombers to help out the Luftwaffe over London. They did not come well out of it since the RAF shot them all down, and the gesture was not repeated. Nevertheless it was known that the Italians were house-trained, in spite of all the Fascist windbaggery, and when not up against such as the Abyssinians, would fight clean. Those unlucky enough to fall into their hands as prisoners could count on civilized treatment. To bomb Berlin would have been a pleasure, especially to those who had seen London, Coventry, Liverpool and a score of other such places as the Luftwaffe had visited. Nobody wanted to bomb Rome.

The RAF alone had earned all the glory going so far by thrashing the German Air Force in English skies. The Army, neglected until the last minute as always, was still waiting for an opportunity to fight its battles with something better than the equivalent of a sharpened stick. Now it was the turn of the Senior Service to put on a performance more effective than that of Keyes at Zeebrugge and give the country a demonstrable victory. It needed one very badly. November is a horrible month at the best of times and during this one the war could hardly have been going worse.

In accordance with Rear-Admiral Lyster's orders, *Illustrious* 'adjusted course and speed to pass through "Position X", [270° and 40 miles from Kabbo Point], at 20.00, when course will be altered into wind and speed adjusted to give a speed of 30 knots.' Four cruisers and the same number of destroyers mounted guard over her. It was a fine night, with a bright three-quarter moon but a lot of low cloud at about 8,000 feet.

By the prescribed time all the dozen Swordfishes, extra tanks crammed in (or, with the bombers, fastened between the wheels) so that their usual range might be doubled, were drawn up on the flight deck. By 20.40 all of them were airborne; by 20.57 they had formed up in 'vics' as a squadron 8 miles from the ship and set a course for Taranto Bay, Williamson and Scarlett leading the torpedo-droppers in L4A. At best they had a flight of five or six hours, broken by a battle, to look forward to. Should any Italian aircraft of almost any fighting capacity put in an appearance the Stringbags, lacking their gunners, would have been cold meat. There was too much to do in plotting and keeping a course of 170 miles to worry about such things. By 21.15 the formation had become ragged with at least one aircraft gone adrift in the clouds. All, listening keenly to the notes of their Pegasus engines, pressed steadily on. Taranto Bay was not hard to find. An American Professor* with the US Geological Survey has recently produced a paper asserting its regular shape to be the work of a meteorite 35 million years ago. It was about to experience a night probably the most animating since that event; certainly, with Swordfishes dancing like mosquitoes round a pressure lamp, the most spectacular.

The RAF had been a good friend to the Navy by making constant visits to the neighbourhood in order to take photographs and generally see what was going on. It had indeed suggested that the entire job might be done by Wellingtons from Malta; as Wellingtons knew nothing of torpedoes the idea did not catch on. What actually took place on the night of the raid was not wholly according to plan. It appears that a Sunderland flying-boat, unconscious of what the Navy was doing, had blundered across the sky half an hour before the arrival of Williamson's raiders and had triggered off the Italian sound detectors. So began the most important naval engagement in the Mediterranean for a very long time.

Charles Lamb flatly denied the official version of the Italian awakening by a peccant Sunderland. He had come to the FAA as mentioned earlier, by devious ways, first from the Merchant Navy and then, unable to find a sea-going berth, by way of the RAF. By the time of the Taranto strike he was 26 years old and a highly experienced practitioner. Because he had been given one of the less important tasks, second flare-dropper, he had a grandstand view of the first strike. His account of the matter is that 'Almost as soon as we were airborne we had to climb through heavy cumulus cloud, and when we emerged into the moonlight at 7,500 feet only nine of the twelve aircrafts' lights were in sight. When the others were unable to find their leader they flew direct to

* (Professor C. Wylie Poag, in *Geology*, August, 1994)

Taranto. One of them was Ian Swayne, who flew at sea level and reached the target area fifteen minutes before anyone else. He had no wish to be the first uninvited guest of the Italian Navy in Taranto, and for a quarter of an hour he flew to and fro, keeping the harbour in sight waiting for the main strike. There was nothing else he could do but, of course, his presence had been detected by the Italian listening devices, and as a result all the harbour defences and the ships had been alerted.'

Whichever plane had been the marplot, the damage was done. For Lyster's plan to have any chance of success surprise was absolutely necessary and now this essential was gone. No participant, of course, seriously expected to swoop down upon a sleeping ship, release his torpedo and disappear into the night listening for the sound of a satisfactory explosion. The complicated web of agents built up by Italy over many years around the whole Mediterranean littoral meant that their Intelligence must have a pretty good idea of the Navy's plans and of its capability. It is more than likely that the 1935 plan, even in its improved form, existed in copy somewhere in Mussolini's Admiralty. The best that could be hoped for, and it was enormously important, was the gift of the first couple of minutes in which to get the work done before the anchored ships and their crews realized what was afoot. It would have been beyond anticipation that the countrymen of Rizzo and Rossetti would be caught off guard simply by a form of attack never tried before. As matters stood the Stringbag torpedo pilots had no choice but to dive into the maelstrom, pick out their targets as best they could, go through the drills they had practised so often and hope for the best.

The bombers, now without the slightest chance of catching the smaller ships, the seaplane base or the oil installations in unguarded postures, must set about them quickly before making themselves scarce. Once Taranto was in sight everything depended upon the skill and determination of each individual pilot. The observer had his work cut out in navigating the machine to the target and, with luck, in navigating it back to the carrier. During the attack his only function was to cling grimly on in his gyrating canvas box, making quite sure of being properly strapped in, watching and, if he felt like it, praying. Nobody envied the observer, for he could see everything and do nothing. It was the quality of the men at the controls that would settle the business and determine whether the Mar Grande was to be decorated with sunken battleships or wrecked Swordfishes. In a cramped area littered with wide-awake gunners manning pieces of every size and half-dazzled by the flashes they must somehow combine perfection of delivery of their weapons with the avoidance of destruction until at least that had been accomplished.

The official account remarks, on the subject of considerations in the minds of the planners, that 'The AA fire likely to be encountered at Taranto was not considered a serious deterrent'.* It certainly did not deter but it was not a factor to be lightly dismissed. Again it is the official version which asserts that 'Not until the flares had been dropped to the East of the *MAR GRANDE* at 2300 did the batteries open a barrage fire against the strike, the light AA weapons on the ships joining in as the torpedo attack was delivered some minutes later'. Lamb remarked something different: 'For the last 15 minutes of our passage across the Ionian Sea Scarlett had no navigational problems, for Taranto could be seen from a distance of 50 miles or more, because of the welcome awaiting us. The sky over the harbour looked as it sometimes does over Mount Etna, in Sicily, when the great volcano erupts. The darkness was being torn apart by a firework display which spat flame into the night to a height of nearly 5,000 feet. "They don't seem very pleased to see us," said Grieve. As he spoke "Blood" Scarlett's dimmed Aldis light flashed the breakaway signal to Kiggell and me, telling us to start adding to the illuminations over the crowded harbour.' It seems hard to contradict the man who writes that 'for an unforgettable half hour I had a bird's eye view of history in the making'. For that Charles Lamb certainly had.

This appears to have been the sequence of events. The Italian gunners in the San Vito area, away to the south-east, opened barrage first at about 22.50 as the first aircraft arrived. Fortunately it was aimed in the wrong direction, away from Williamson and the rest. Two minutes later the flare-droppers were detached and made their way eastward, either through or over the balloon barrage. By 13.02 Kiggell and Janvrin in L4P had laid their line of parachute flares, 4,500 feet up and half a mile apart, neatly

---

* The Staff appreciation actually prophesied a casualty rate of 50 per cent.

silhouetting the battleships for the torpedo-droppers. Each flare had a delay action of 1,000 feet before it ignited and the high-angle guns, more interested in bagging these than in anything else, hit nothing. Their tracer shells, known still by the First War name of 'flaming onions', gave fair warning of approach to anything as agile as a Swordfish.

From his position of advantage Lamb saw the entire performance by the first strike, and a fearsome sight it was. 'Before the first Swordfish had dived to the attack, the full-throated roar from the guns of six battleships and the blast from the cruisers and destroyers made the harbour defences seem like a side-show.' Into this volcanic eruption of flame and steel the Fleet Air Arm had to descend. It seemed to the observers above beyond belief that anything could not be ripped to shreds by the sheer volume of the fire, however ill-directed it might be.

The leader arrived at the harbour entrance precisely as Kiggell's first flare burst into a cloud of yellow light, so brilliant that it turned the blue-grey camouflage of Williamson's aircraft into a shining white. Lamb watched it dive from 5,000 feet to sea level, below the flak, and quickly lost sight of what came next. Along with Sparke and Neale in L4C and Macaulay and Wray in L4R Williamson and Scarlett came in over the batteries at 4,000 feet and instantly went into a dive. Their target was *Cavour* and to come within torpedo range of her it would have been necessary to fly between the cables of the balloons to the south-west of the battleship anchorage, over the mole named Diga di Tarantola followed immediately by releasing. Then their luck ran out. In the words of the official report, after explaining how they had flown to the centre of the Mar Grande, 'This was the last seen of L4A by the British. The aircraft was sighted in the path of the moon diving at high speed with the engine cut out at 23.14 by the destroyer *Fulmine*, which at once opened fire at about 1,000 yards range. L4A's torpedo, dropped from a height of about 30 feet, narrowly missed the *Fulmine* and hit the *Cavour*. The aircraft then crashed near the floating dock. Both officers were rescued by the Italians and made prisoners of war.'

That is the official version. Scarlett did not put it in quite the same way. He was not wholly convinced that whilst turning in the middle of the harbour in order to make their getaway they had been shot down at all. 'We put a wing-tip in the water. I couldn't tell. I just fell out of the back into the sea. We were only about 20 feet up. It wasn't very far to drop. I never tie myself in on these occasions. Then old Williamson came up a bit later on and we hung about by the aircraft which still had its tail sticking out of the water. Chaps ashore were shooting at it. The water was boiling so I swam off to a floating dock and climbed on board that. We didn't know we'd done any good with our torpedoes. Thought we might have, because they all looked a bit long in the face, the Wops.'

They had, indeed, hit *Cavour* fair and square, the only aircraft in the strike to achieve a result so lethal. *Cavour* died of wounds. A hole 40 feet by 27 on the port bow was fatal. Though beached and abandoned immediately, she was firmly on the bottom by breakfast time on the following day. One has to hope that Scarlett was satisfied. He was a reluctant aviator, press-ganged in 1937 as an observer when, as he said, 'I wanted to be in destroyers, not bloody aeroplanes'. By the time approval came through for his transfer back to general service, following an application made in the old *Glorious* days, 'Blood' Scarlett was busily engaged in being a model prisoner of war. He developed such a talent for infuriating guards that he was turned over to the Germans. In 1945 he was the instigator of an attempt to escape from a camp at Lübeck for which he was Mentioned in Despatches. The ducking probably saved his life; few of the forty who flew to Taranto lived for long afterwards.

The two other aircraft in the sub-flight could not be expected to repeat such a success. L4C, piloted by Sub-Lieutenant (A) P.J.D. Sparke, and L4R with Sub-Lieutenant A.S.D. Macaulay at the controls both crossed the Diga di Tarantola at about the same 30 feet as their leader had done and looked for victims. This was not as easy as it may sound. Sparke was after the flagship *Vittorio Veneto*, moored a little to the north of the point at which the two survivors of Williamson's sub-flight loosed their torpedoes and swung 180 degrees round to return by the same way that they had come. Much nearer, almost underneath them as they made the turn and firing with every machine gun she possessed, was the recently arrived and not yet hit *Cavour*. Sparke, under the impression that he was aiming for the flagship, let slip his torpedo at

Cavour from a range of about 700 yards. Macaulay followed suit. Neither torpedo found a mark. The watch aboard *Andrea Doria*, a little to *Cavour*'s north-east, reported two bombs as having exploded near her at 23.15. Since no bombs were dropped at or near that time and place it seems a safe assumption that the noises came from the wasted torpedoes of L4C and L4R. Both crews were back on the flight deck of *Illustrious* a little before 01.30, touching down within five minutes of each other. Only three torpedoes remained of the six with which the First Striking Force had set off.

The other flight of torpedo-bombers occupied themselves with ships in the northern half of the Mar Grande. Swayne's L4M, as you know, had been hanging about the harbour mouth for a quarter of an hour waiting for their turn. On seeing Kiggell's flares beginning to light the place up at 23.02, Swayne and Buscall crossed the submerged breakwater at 1,000 feet and streaked across the centre of the Mar Grande losing height all the time. At 23.15 they made out the shape of a large battleship, *Littorio*, and turned sharply to port, bringing her into the torpedo sight. L4M's missile needed no Duplex pistol. It struck *Littorio* on the port quarter and exploded satisfactorily. This was not *Littorio*'s only misfortune, for she was as unlucky as her sister *Vittorio Veneto* had been the reverse. Almost at the same moment as Swayne struck her aft another torpedo hit the starboard bow. This came from L4K, the Swordfish of Lieutenant Kemp. He had steered a course well to the north of the others, following the coastline of the Mar Grande to the entrance to the inner harbour; there he had made his swing southwards, under intense AA fire of all kinds, and let drive at a range of about 1,000 yards.

Eagle's aircraft, E4F, Lieutenants Maund and Bull, came in from an even further northerly direction but soon picked up and followed Kemp. E4F was the unlucky one. Her torpedo, dropped very near to Kemp's 'grounded short and exploded harmlessly'. Thus were all six torpedoes of the First Striking Force accounted for. All the Swordfishes made their ways safely home, Bailey noting carefully that he had seen several shells from the anchored cruisers hitting their own merchantmen.

These aircraft had survived not merely a very heavy bombardment by AA guns of all shapes and sizes but they had run the risk, by no means negligible, of entangling themselves in the forests of balloon cables. A conversation, possibly apocryphal but still credible, has passed into folklore. Pilot to observer: 'Where's that bloody balloon barrage?' Observer to pilot: 'We've been through it once and we're just going through it again.' Another conversation, firmly attributable, survives also. Charles Lamb and his observer, Lieutenant K.C. Grieve, were making their way back each seriously believing that their L5B might well be the only Swordfish to have come through. Lamb, having said through the Gosport Tube what they were both thinking, added that 'All the top brass will want to know exactly what happened and whether the attack was a success and how many hits were scored and so on, and if we are the only survivors they will expect us to know. Frankly, I saw nothing, apart from the flak which covered the whole harbour. I couldn't see beyond it. Did you see whether Neil Kemp and company got any hits?' Grieve, plainly not a great talker, answered, 'You were throwing the aircraft about like a madman half the time, and every time I tried to look over the side the slipstream nearly whipped off my goggles! The harbour was blanked out by ack-ack and I had to check with the compass to see which way we were facing.' In all probability every observer might have said something like it.

Lamb, the excitement over, meditated for a moment. 'On the way back from these parties I always breathed a small prayer of thanks that I was not an observer,' he wrote many years later. 'Their responsibilities ended at the target until it was time to go home again, and then they had to be very cool-headed and accurate and do difficult sums. When the excitement was at its height all they could do was sit tight and pray.' There can hardly be room for two opinions about that; but observers might well have had something much the same, though with obvious variations, to say about their pilots.

Time was soon to show that the understandable feelings of gloom were based on no foundation. The first striking force was not doing at all badly. The torpedo carriers were, of course, the heavy cavalry but there was work enough for the others. The bombers were badly let down by their equipment, but that they had as yet no reason to know.

Three aircraft, E5A, E5Q and L4H, had been given the

secondary task of bombing such ships as they could find and, for good measure, the unmissable oil fuel depot. There was no shortage of targets. On the Italian Navy's own official figures, the Mar Grande housed six battleships, three heavy cruisers and eight destroyers; in the Mar Piccolo there were two more heavy cruisers moored to buoys, two more along with two smaller ones lying bow and stern to the wharf like yachts on the riviera; twenty-one more destroyers, five torpedo boats, sixteen submarines, nine tankers and a good many smaller fry shared what should have been the safety of this enclosed basin. The Italian fleet in Taranto was far from negligible.

The most experienced pilot was Captain 'Ollie' Patch of the Royal Marines. At 26 and already with a DSO for his part in the Bomba Bay affair, he was one of the senior men and his observer, Lieutenant Goodwin, was even older. E5A* arrived over San Pietro island a couple of minutes after the flare-droppers, having become separated on the way. On arrival Patch was conscious of some disappointment, for 'there was nothing much happening'. Such account as he gave to posterity, in the same way as Scarlett, was preserved in his obituary. Before very long he was 'diving down through a hail of anti-aircraft fire and a wonderful Brock's benefit of tracer and searchlights'. These last probably came from the ships in the Mar Piccolo in which he was interesting himself. The multiplicity of targets was confusing, a confusion not helped by the volume of fire from heavy machine guns that all seemed to be directed at him as the Swordfish crossed the inner harbour from north-west to south-east. The two heavy cruisers at buoys – they would have been *Trieste* and *Bolzano* – looked the most deserving and Patch set about dive-bombing them. It does not seem that any of the bombs connected with their targets; probably this was no great matter for, according to the Italians, few of the bombs dropped that night exploded anyway. Once they had been dropped, however, Patch and Goodwin had to make their escape from the furthest point reached by anybody. The evasive action needed was violent, so much so that 'his observer sitting behind him was thrown out of his seat and but for the "monkey's tail" wire that secured him to the aircraft, would have gone straight

* All the aircraft prefixed with the letter E came from HMS *Eagle*.

overboard'. Patch, having evaded one battery by dodging behind a hill, rather cleverly took his machine low down over the roofs of the citizens of Taranto, 'unmolested except for one horrid little man firing at us'. E5A then steered a highly individual course eight miles to the east of the town and arrived safely home at 01.35.

As the other two bomber crews were less fortunate in their obituarists they have less corroborative detail. Their bravery went unrewarded. Consider L4H, the Swordfish of the young Sub-Lieutenants Forde and Mardel-Ferreira, one of the four RNVR officers there. They too attacked heavy cruisers in the Mar Piccolo and hit nothing; but read slowly this bald statement: 'First bomb fell in water short of the two 8-inch cruisers. During the dive intense AA fire was suffered. The pilot was not sure that his bombs had dropped, so turned round in the western part of the Mar Piccolo and repeated the attack'. 'Best traditions of the Navy' can be a joke expression; not always.

The last bomber, *Eagle*'s E5Q, had good cause to grumble. The aircraft, manned by Lieutenant Murray and Sub-Lieutenant Paine, arrived to the eastward of Cape San Vito just as the flares were beginning to burn. Then they carried out a systematic attack with their four bombs along the line of moored ships at the wharf-side, maintaining a steady height of 3,000 feet. By good luck, excellent judgment or both they dropped one of their 250-lb semi-armour piercing bombs squarely on the destroyer *Libeccio*. The next sentence almost writes itself. The bomb failed to go off and two disgusted naval officers flew back to their carrier.

Kemp's observer, Bailey, had mentioned seeing a fire burning in 'the vicinity of the seaplane base'. This would have been the work of the most junior combatants of all, Sub-Lieutenant Sarra and Mr Midshipman Bowker in L4L. Their approach had been made at a much higher level, for they were bombers not torpedo-launchers. L4L came in over Cape Rondinella – it means 'little swallow' – at about 8,000 feet, dived over the Mar Grande down to 1500, hotly pursued by every sort of gunfire, and looked to see what they could most profitably bomb. Hardly surprisingly Bowker found himself unable to choose between such a multi-plicity of targets and, being a sensible young man, he directed his driver to the seaplane base. The result was more satisfactory than with most of the bombings. All of them exploded and the hangar and slipway were hit as well as 'a storehouse which blew up with a loud explosion'. These were, presumably, the buildings and installations so carefully put up by the RNAS in 1917. The young men had more than their share of luck. On landing, they counted seventeen bullet holes in their Stringbag, more than any other had suffered save only for Wellham, whose turn was yet to come.

The second pair of flare-droppers were amongst the last away. Lamb, astern of Kiggell and Janvrin and with little to do, persuaded himself that he was in no danger but that every one of the torpedo-droppers must have been smashed to pieces. Having obediently bombed the oil installations, with about as much success as the others, he defiantly and rudely excreted his flares one by one in order to give the Italians something more upon which to waste ammunition. He and Grieve flew unhappily back to *Illustrious* firmly convinced, as has been already told, that they were the only survivors.

So ended the foray of the First Striking Force. All save the leader were back on board by 02.00 with not so much as a burst tyre between them. The damage inflicted consisted of two torpedo hits on *Littorio*, one on *Cavour* and a heavy piece of pig-iron and explosive dropped on *Libeccio*. The cost was one Swordfish and two officers, missing believed killed.

After the various mishaps to aircraft already related, it can hardly come as a surprise that the Second Striking Force was smaller than originally planned. It came close to being smaller still. L5F had very nearly lost her observer before the operation began. Early on the morning of the 11th, when on a routine patrol, the Swordfish then carrying him had force landed in the sea some 20 miles distant from *Illustrious*. Going and his telegraphist-airgunner had been shot over the nose, head-first into the water, picked up by the cruiser *Gloucester* and flown home in her 'Shagbat' – Walrus amphibian. The ducking was no deterrent, though it did once more make the point that open-cockpit aircraft still had their advantages. Going remarked that 'it was a most comfortable way to ditch, no pain being suffered by anyone'. The observation suggests meiosis. Going had no intention of being left out of the main business, as later events were to show.

The second flight began to take off at 21.23, as Williamson's squadron was somewhere near the half-way mark. All that could be mustered was five machines carrying torpedoes, two bombers and two more doubling as bombers and flare-droppers. As the Swordfish's bomb load counted six apiece for the bombers proper and two for the flare-droppers they did not add up to anything very formidable on that score. Once more the torpedo launchers were the grandees of the operation. There could be no question of a second surprise attack. Even if the defenders were not expecting to be hit a second time they would have recovered from the first shock and been very ready to open up with every weapon they had. No member of the second strike crews could have thought otherwise. It was not a deterrent.

The nine aircraft detailed for the task looked like being reduced to eight even before becoming airborne. Lieutenant Going, you will remember, had already had one watery experience that day. When he and his pilot, Lieutenant Clifford, were told that something had gone amiss with one of the 250-lb bombs their Swordfish was carrying they could quite honourably have taken no part in the operation. They took another view of the matter. Speaking, one may fairly infer, unkindly to those whose fault it had been, Clifford and Going insisted on the damage being put to rights even if it would mean their being late for the fair. Work was instantly put in hand. Hardly believably it was all finished within 25 minutes.

The remaining eight took off at 23.50, almost exactly a quarter of an hour after the last machine of the first strike had left the scene of action. The outward-bound adventures were not over yet. A short distance from *Illustrious*, while still jilling about awaiting the march off in formation, L5Q, the aircraft of Lieutenant Morford and Sub-Lieutenant Green, met with misfortune. The external overload petrol tank, badly secured in some fashion, fell off. The fittings began to bang against the fuselage. With fuel only for half the journey and unknown damage done the crew had no choice but to return. It was not a contingency for which plans had been made. On approaching *Illustrious* Green fired a red Very light. Those on board plainly regarded this as a hostile act; *Illustrious* opened fire, soon to be joined by *Berwick*. It was no more effective than usual. A two-star identification light made all things clear, the firing stopped and two crestfallen young officers climbed down on to the carrier's deck. To compensate for their loss, for L5Q had also been a bomber, Clifford and Going, faint but pursuing, caught up with the others after a loss of 24 minutes' flying time just as the battle was beginning.

The torpedo-carriers flew in to the north of cape Rondinella, keeping well away from the batteries on San Pietro island. The design was for each to cross the Mar Grande along its northern shore diving sharply from 5,000 feet to about 30, loosing the torpedoes at the battleships and returning to sea on a parallel course to the south. The flare-droppers would have arrived from a diametrically opposite position, over Cape San Vito and once more coming between the battleships and the moon. The two Swordfishes involved, L5B (Lieutenant Hamilton and Sub-Lieutenant Weekes) and L4F, (Lieutenant Skelton and Sub-Lieutenant Perkins) experienced no great difficulty in carrying out their share. That done, with lines of brightness burning along the east and south-east of the Mar Grande, they followed the examples of their precursors and set about the oil installations with bombs; 'it was thought unsuccessfully,' Perkins honestly reported. They could, however, stake a claim to a small fire.

Moments later the torpedo launchers swept over Cape Rondinella and dived over the merchant ship harbour under an intense barrage. The leader, Hale and Carline in L5A, in close company with L5H, (Lieutenant Lea and Sub-Lieutenant Jones) and E4H (Lieutenants Bayly and Slaughter), all went for the *Littorio*, still suffering from the first strike's attentions. E4H suddenly veered to starboard, across the path of the other two, and either exploded in mid-air or crashed into the sea. It is the general belief based on the official Italian account that the aircraft was attempting to hit not the battleship but the cruiser *Gorizia*; a torpedo was later found floating in the outer harbour with its striking head crushed but the warhead undetonated. It can hardly have come from anywhere else. Slaughter and Bayly were never seen alive again.

Hale and the team led by his L5K enjoyed better fortune. Michael Torrens-Spence had been described by a brother officer as one of the Navy's most accomplished aviators. 'Tiffy', as his friends called him, was an Ulsterman, a maintenance test pilot and second in command of 819 Squadron. Charles Lamb had written that, during the Greek campaign, he was to bring the Italian cruiser *Pola* to a standstill with his single torpedo. When the Italian captain was rescued from his sinking ship by the destroyer *Jervis* he observed, with emotion, that 'Either that pilot is mad or he is the bravest man in the world'.* It was well known in the wardroom, says Lamb, that Torrens-Spence, by reason of an innate nervousness, would push home any attack almost to the point of suicide. On the night of Taranto he and his leader swooped down together round the northern line of the balloons and inside the nets. Their torpedoes dropped almost simultaneously from a point about 700 yards north of the anchored and already wounded *Littorio*. Both observers told of intense AA fire of all kinds from battleships, cruisers and the shore batteries. One torpedo scored a palpable hit on *Littorio*'s starboard bow, the time of the explosion being exactly logged as 00.01. Nobody will ever know, nor probably now care very much, whether this one or another torpedo found stuck in the mud under the battleship's keel came from the leader. Just this once the Duplex pistol seems to have failed.

The Italian flagship *Vittorio Veneto* came through the whole affair without a scratch. It seems, though certainty is not possible, that the torpedo released during the First Strike by Williamson's wingman, Lieutenant Sparke in L4C, was intended for her even though it is recorded simply as having missed *Cavour*. The flagship's luck held out through the Second Strike even when she became the target of one of *Eagle*'s best pilots, Lieutenant (A) J.W.G. Wellham, DSC, in E5H.† Like the others, he flew in over Cape Rondinella at about 8,000 feet and followed his leader down through the flak. As he did so the first of the flares burst out to the eastward and the fire from the ground grew even more fierce. Wellham, having lost sight of the other aircraft, chose what

---

* In the Imperial War Museum there is a letter from Captain (as he then was) Manley Power to his wife in which he tells of how he tried to calm down this unlucky officer who was threatening suicide. It seems that the shame of having been stopped in his tracks by a Stringbag had been too much for him.

† For a fuller account of the exploits of E5H and her crew see Wellham's *With Naval Wings*, Spellmount Press, 1995. He had won his DSC in the Bomba Bay affair.

seemed a hole in the pattern of red, yellow and green tracer that streamed around his aircraft and dived steeply with speed building up to 170 knots. Then E5H met with misfortune. Having escaped damage from every sort of gunfire she collided with a masterless barrage balloon that had been cut adrift by some means or other. As E5H began to plunge down into the middle of Taranto city, almost unmanageable from the damage she had taken, Wellham fought with the controls in order to make sure that his machine would survive and his torpedo would do something useful. Over his right shoulder loomed the bulk of a great ship – *Vittorio Veneto* herself – and she in turn had seen E5H. Through fire even greater than anything before, since the battleship's guns of all kinds were setting about him, Wellham managed to make a turn of 180 degrees and, with one wing dragging, let drive with his torpedo, made a vertical turn to starboard, and sped off almost across the water.* Later investigation showed that the rod connecting the ailerons on the port side upper and lower wings had been smashed and the jagged ends were grinding together, leaving one aileron up and the other down. Add a large hole in the lower main plane on the same side and one may understand why the Fleet Air Arm insists so firmly that no other aircraft could stand such knocking about. Nor was the quality of pilots behind; only men of Wellham's skill, experience and doggedness could have brought his Stringbag home in such a state. If any aircraft deserved to have scored a torpedo hit it was E5H. But none was recorded. Pat Humphreys, the observer, exhibited a sang-froid worthy of the occasion and of himself, bringing them home to a spectacular landing on *Illustrious* at a few minutes before 3 a.m.

There were to be further victims to the second striking force. Lieutenant Lea and Sub-Lieutenant Jones, the last of the torpedo men, brought L5H over Cape Rondinella between the two aircraft which were to go for *Vittorio Veneto*. Peeling off at about the

---

* In a letter to the author dated 28 November, 1994, Lieutenant-Commander Wellham remarked, 'My own approach, as you will see from the chart, was quite unintentional as I had been hit by flak during the dive and knocked out of control; by the time that I had retrieved the situation I was over Taranto town and so was obliged to deal with the situation in a manner that had never been my intention.'

same spot, hard by the Mar Piccolo entrance, they launched their torpedo at the battleship *Duilio* from about 600 yards. It struck her on the starboard side, abreast No 2 turret, at a depth of 29½ feet. It was not the moment to enquire further about the damage caused. Lea and Jones were off across San Pietro pursued by 'violent fire from cruisers, destroyers and shore batteries'. They, too, were untouched.

Lastly came the laggard L5F of Clifford and Going. They had set a slightly different course and arrived from the far, or eastern, side of the harbour. After circling around the Mar Piccolo entrance they were rewarded with the sight of all the neatly parked cruisers and destroyers lined up against the wharf like cigarettes in a case. Their gunners in turn had seen L5F and set about making life difficult for her. It does not appear that they hit anything; the British armament factories saved them. A bomb hit the cruiser *Trento* very satisfactorily. It failed to explode. Other bombs narrowly missed destroyers, near enough to have damaged their thin plating had they gone off. The official account observes it to have been 'a poor reward for his [Clifford's] bravery'. Possibly he and Going put it in other words. By about 3 o'clock in the morning all but the two casualties were home, unscathed but very tired. They had little enough idea of what they had achieved and were not able to give any detailed account of the damage done. Until fresh photographs came in from the RAF it was possible only to wonder whether or not the whole business had been as Lamb said on the way to the briefing room: 'It looks as though we made a complete cock of it tonight, which is why we've got to go back again. But I don't see how it can be any better on a second attempt. Rather the reverse.'

Certainly it looked as if Admiral Cunningham was going to insist upon another try. Orders had been given for the fitters and riggers to have their machines ready for a second assault and it all sounded deadly serious. One officer was heard to remark that even the Light Brigade hadn't been told to do it again. This may well have been near the mark. How could anything worth while be done without a large butcher's bill? The Light Brigade had been almost wiped out; the Fleet Air Arm had had no more casualties than were sustained on a Bank Holiday Monday on the Brighton road. The weather scotched any attempt at repetition.

There are confused signals about the proposed second run-in. Admiral Cunningham in his Memoirs asserts that 'The aircrews were in a state of great jubilation. They clamoured to repeat the operation the same night. I agreed at first when Rear-Admiral Lyster made the suggestion, though I rather felt that when the excitement wore off and the strain of their ordeal began to tell upon the aircrews it would be unfair to send them in again. I therefore felt somewhat relieved when a bad weather report automatically put a stop to a second venture.' Lieutenant Lamb and his brother officers would have found this surprising. When he made his remark about not seeing how it could be done better at a second attempt, 'Grieve answered my words with a look of sickened dismay'.

The Paymaster Commander, having fortified Lamb with an enormous whisky and soda and asked what he thought of the 'Welcome Home' sign put up by the stewards, received the answer, 'I shall be more pleased to see it this time tomorrow'. The Paymaster Commander, plainly a man of excellent judgment, replied, 'Drink that and you'll feel better. Then have another. I've got a feeling in my water that none of you will be going back. Want to take a bet on it?' Lamb took it. 'That was one bet I was very relieved to lose.' Sir Andrew did acknowledge the bravery, skill and determination by a signal to *Illustrious* that has become history: 'Manoeuvre well executed'. One can not avoid the feeling that Admiral Riccardi would have phrased it better.

The photographs taken by the faithful RAF as soon as the light thinned brought strong evidence that no second attack would have been needed. The results of the first looked very satisfactory indeed.

Consider for a moment the gauntlet that the aircrews had had to run. Taranto was a naval base of the first order, equivalent in its own way to Portsmouth or Wilhelmshaven. Naturally enough it was furnished with guns of all shapes and sizes in profusion. There were batteries on San Pietro island, where the harbour entrance was partially blocked, floating batteries along the submerged breakwaters on either side of the island, at intervals around the harbour perimeter and, just to make sure no gaps had been left, on pontoons moored at four points in the Mar Grande. The returns of ammunition expended on this November night fell

114

into the hands of the Royal Navy after the Italian surrender. They give a total figure of 13,489 rounds, roughly two-thirds being shells from cannon of more than 3" calibre and the remainder dispensed by machine guns of all sizes.

The Italian records are confined to shore batteries alone but contain the remark that 'Ships' gunfire was confined to machine guns; expenditure is unknown'. This sounds less than likely. The battleships and cruisers alone carried many heavy weapons – the Cavours carried eighteen AA guns of more than 3" calibre and the Littorios a dozen each – and Charles Lamb was quite firm that it was the ships' guns that contributed most to the volume. It is improbable that any exact figure of rounds blazed away will ever be put together now, certainly in the tally of small arms ammunition; nor does it greatly matter. There were enough projectiles covering the harbour to have shredded every Swordfish had they been better directed. Not unreasonably the heavier pieces were turned on the flares. Bring them down and the aircraft would be blinded. The time lag between the dropping and the ignition was, however, too great for artillery successes. Neither flare nor dropper was touched.

Other guns began by firing lines of shells so low that they seemed to be hitting each other. That discovered, they lifted their sights and provided an umbrella of flame and steel under which the Swordfishes flew unscathed. Had the gunners continued to fire low, at water level, they could hardly have failed to hit some or all of the torpedo-droppers. All of these, save of course Williamson and Bayly, made their way back scarcely at all above the level of the sea; Michael Torrens-Spence actually bounced off the water as he came through the harbour entrance with wheels partly submerged. The reason for firing barrages at that altitude was obvious. At any other, many shells would have hit the town and probably as many would have found their targets on Italian ships. Kemp, of L4K, says firmly that 'Several shells from the cruisers were seen to hit merchant ships in harbour'.

It would have required something exceptional in the way of gunnery procedures to have achieved much against the torpedo-droppers once each had finished its run-in. The lower a 'fish' can be dropped the better, and performance is much improved once the weight of nearly 2,000 lbs has gone. The attacks made by

Williamson's flight lasted only five minutes from arrival to departure, except only for Williamson's L4A. The bombers, higher up and there for longer, would have made more rewarding targets.

Then comes the matter of searchlights. No pilot reported having encountered any. The concensus of opinion on their return was that the Italians had thus deprived themselves of a possibly good bag. Ian Swayne is quoted by Lamb as having expressed the opinion that, had they used their lights, they would have shot down every single aircraft. Lamb, from his position of advantage, disagreed vehemently: 'From above I could see that the opposite was the case; because the aircraft were only a few feet above sea level, the use of searchlights would have floodlit the six battleships and the harbour defences, and greatly assisted the attacking aircraft in selecting their target.' He adds that 'From my position astern of Kiggell and Janvrin I was in no danger whatever and could watch proceedings at leisure. I have never been in less danger in any attack than I was that night, when the rest of the squadron were flying into the jaws of hell. I was convinced that none of the torpedoing aircraft could have survived.'

Whatever the benefits or otherwise of searchlight activity for the defenders, it seems that the failure to use them was caused by consternation rather than fire plan. The report of the Italian Commander-in-Chief Afloat to the Chief of Naval Staff, compiled after the attack, is specific enough. Under the heading 'Defence of Anchorage', it reads:- 'Defence of outer anchorage from air attack was arranged as follows:-

Shore batteries (4.09-inch, 4.02-inch and 3.05-inch).
Stations ashore and afloat, of machine guns (0.8-inch and 1.6-inch) were specially detailed to engage torpedo aircraft. 'Photo-electrics', ashore and on pontoons, could intercept on moonlight nights either bombers or torpedo aircraft, according to arrangements made by Central Control.
    The part to be played by ships at anchor was as follows:-
No barrage fire at the same time as the shore batteries.
Machine guns to be manned and fired with the main armament against aircraft visible to the naked eye or illuminated by searchlight.

On moonlight nights two searchlights a ship to work with those of the shore batteries in previously defined sectors, for defence against torpedo aircraft. These had to be integrated with the searchlights worked by the base.'

Nobody could accuse the Italian authorities of not trying. The plan did not work out as had been hoped. Such has happened to nations other than Italy at most times throughout recorded history. The report ends, a touch plaintively, with an assertion that recent enemy air activity had 'served as a warning of heavy air attacks'. Against aircraft less acrobatic than the Stringbag and pilots of lesser quality than these the Italians might have enjoyed better fortune.

8

DEBITS AND CREDITS

M r Churchill, in accordance with his nature, expressed a view rather more generous than that of the Admiral. On the day after the Stringbags, less two, had returned to the nest he stood up in Parliament and spoke with feeling. The Prime Minister deserved his opportunity after months and months of nothing but failure and defeat to report. He took it. 'I have some news for the House. It is good news. The Royal Navy has struck a crippling blow at the Italian fleet. The total strength of the Italian battle fleet was six battleships, two of them of the "Littorio" class, which have just been put into service and are, of course, among the most powerful vessels in the world and four of the recently reconstructed "Cavour" class. This fleet was, to be sure, considerably more powerful on paper than our Mediterranean Fleet, but it had consistently refused to accept battle. On the night of the 11th–12th November, when the main units of the Italian fleet were lying behind their shore defences in their naval base at Taranto, our aircraft of the Fleet Air Arm attacked them in their stronghold.'

He went on, not without relish, to set out in some detail all that the photographs rushed to him by the RAF had depicted. His exposition was as accurate as it could be from photographs alone. 'It is now established that one battleship of the "Littorio" class was badly down by the bows and that her forecastle is under water and she has a heavy list to starboard. One battleship of the "Cavour" class has been beached, and her stern, up to and including the turret, is under water. This ship is also heavily listed to starboard. It has not yet been possible to establish the fact with certainty, but it appears that a second battleship of the "Cavour" class has also been severely damaged and beached.* In the inner harbour of Taranto two Italian cruisers are listed to starboard and are surrounded with oil fuel, and two fleet auxiliaries are lying with their sterns under water. The Italian communique of 12th November, in admitting that one warship had been severely damaged, claimed that six of our aircraft had been shot down and three more probably. In fact only two of our aircraft are missing, and it is noted that the enemy claimed that part of the crews had been taken prisoner. I felt it my duty to bring this glorious episode to the immediate notice of the House. As the result of a determined and highly successful attack, which reflects the greatest honour on the Fleet Air Arm, only three Italian battleships remain effective.'†

The Prime Minister went on to speak of heroism of a more customary kind, the loss of the *Jervis Bay* along with Captain Fogarty Fegen and his entire ship's company, sunk by the German battleship she had taken on in a hopeless, valiant, attack in order to give her convoy some chance to get away. It was the first time since the purely defensive Battle of Britain that Mr Churchill had been able to speak of hitting back, and hitting back hard. Along with the entire nation, he made the most of it.

It took some days before a proper assessment of the damage could be made. *Littorio*, though looking dramatic with two naval auxiliaries, a large submarine, a tanker and several smaller craft close alongside, was not desperately hurt, certainly not for a ship fairly struck by three torpedoes. The two hits scored by the first strike had holed her. Neil Kemp's hit on the starboard bow had blown an opening 49 by 32 feet in the bulge abreast No 1 6-inch turret; that from Ian Swayne in L4M had opened up another on the port quarter, 23 feet by 5, abreast the tiller flat. The second strike, that of Torrens-Spence in L5K, had been the most damaging. The torpedo had struck home at a very low level on the starboard side, forward of Kemp's hit, blowing a hole 40 feet

* It had.

† His letter to President Roosevelt of the 21st includes 'Duplex pistols were used, and probably contributed to the success of the torpedo attack'.

by 30. Less importantly, the fourth torpedo was found in the mud under *Littorio*'s stern – there was an unaccountable dent in her starboard quarter – with its striking cap damaged by impact after passing the target. Praise is due to Engineer Inspector-General Umberto Pugliese and the Ansaldo company for designing and building a ship strong enough to survive such punishment. *Littorio*, down by the bows and with her forecastle awash, retired hurt. She was, however, capable of repair and was back at sea by the end of the following March. Perhaps the 18" torpedo, even with the Duplex fuse, was not the ultimate weapon for use against battleships and their like.

The older ships, *Cavour* and *Duilio*, were in a worse plight. Williamson's torpedo had made the biggest impression of them all, leaving a hole 40 feet by 27 on the port bow under the fore-most turret. Two oil fuel tanks were flooded, and only with difficulty were the adjacent compartments prevented from flood-ing as well. L4A, whatever the fate of its occupants, had delivered a knock-out punch. At 05.45 *Cavour* was towed inshore and abandoned, settling comfortably down with her stern on the bot-tom. Almost all her decks were under water, the after turret submerged entirely. She was refloated in July, 1941, and towed to Trieste but for the *Conte di Cavour* the war was over. She never came back.

Duilio was the victim of L5H in the second striking force. 'Sprog' Lea's torpedo had made a clean hit on the starboard side at a depth of 29 ft 6 in and blown a gap 36 feet by 23 between Nos 1 and 2 magazines. Both were completely flooded. Like her sister, *Caio Duilio* was beached, patched up and towed to Genoa. Repairs took until the end of May, 1941.

The Official Report rounds it off: 'The results of the bombing attacks were not noticeable at the time. It is now known that the *Trento* and *Libeccio* received direct hits from bombs which failed to explode, and other ships were narrowly missed; according to the Italians, few of these bombs exploded.' This was a dis-appointment of some order. Ranged alongside at the destroyer/ cruiser quay complex had been twenty-one destroyers and large torpedo boats with four cruisers berthed bow and stern along a frontage of no more than 1,000 yards. Had that not been target enough there were three more destroyers and two more heavy cruisers just offshore. The two bombs out of two dozen that hit but failed to explode caused a small amount of damage – the RAF photographs show a quantity of leaked oil on the surface of the Mar Piccolo – but it was a disproportionate reward for so much skill, determination and plain old-fashioned courage. The lesson it was supposed to have taught, but which was shown a couple of months later to have been dreadfully wrong, was that the bomb was almost worthless as a means of sinking ships even at anchor. In all forty-two of them, of the standard 250-lb SAP pattern, fused nose and tail, were dropped.

The oil tanks suffered some damage, judging from the fires seen to start, but it can not have amounted to much. More important was the attack on the seaplane base. This was home to the spotters which plagued Cunningham's fleet and radioed back every move made by every ship. It took six bombs, direct hits on hangar and slipway, with a satisfactorily large fire caused in the adjacent building. Wellham knew it to be still smouldering on the following day. The result would not, of course, have been to put the spotters out of business but it can not have been helpful to them.

Far and away the most important consequence was the moral effect. Taranto raised the hearts of everybody on the allied side, as a demonstration that we had moved on from the 'Britain Can Take It' slogans and posters of some months earlier. At last it was plain that Britain was beginning to acquire the ability to dish it out. The Italian navy had not seemed exactly avid to come to hand-grips with Cunningham's ships even when they outnumbered and outgunned them handsomely. Now that the strength of the Italian battlefleet had been halved and the Royal Navy strengthened by another battleship, three cruisers and two destroyers, the light of battle in the eyes of the Duce's sailors grew no fiercer. Small blame to them.

That the episode had been glorious was beyond question and it had come at a moment when glorious episodes were a little scarce. Even making all allowances for the general mood towards the end of a year not notable for victories, it may have been that the results were not entirely what they ought to have been. Had surprise been achieved there might have been some chance of sinking the prime targets. *Vittorio Veneto* and *Littorio*, roughly equivalent to the Royal Navy's *Prince of Wales* and *Duke of York*, got off lightly. *Littorio* was removed from the scene for a matter of months only; two torpedoes were aimed at *Vittorio Veneto*, one grounding harmlessly and the other missing altogether. Of the two older ships, comparable with *Royal Oak* and *Royal Sovereign, Cavour* had been eliminated from the war and *Duilio* taken out of it for half a year. Fortune had not favoured Operation Judgment, but it would have been worthwhile for the moral effect alone. 'Glorious Episode' was not mere hyperbole.

Fraternal greetings came from a namesake to HMS *Eagle*: 'The American Eagle Club of London expresses hearty admiration of your gallant work at Taranto. Americans abroad and at home will be proud of you. Congratulations. Robert H. Hutchinson, chairman.' No message came from another navy whose creation had been largely the work of the Lords Commissioners of the Admiralty. Admiral Yamamoto doubtless studied the operation in detail, for it contained practical experience that would come in useful a little over a year later. Nobody expected praise from that quarter.

Captain Boyd of *Illustrious* addressed his ship's company, pointing out that 'in one night the ship's aircraft had achieved a greater amount of damage to the enemy than Nelson had achieved in the Battle of Trafalgar, and nearly twice the amount that the entire British fleet achieved in the Battle of Jutland in the First World War'. Had he felt so inclined, Captain Boyd might have parodied Admiral Beatty's much-quoted remark on that occasion: 'There's something wrong with our bloody bombs today, Chatfield.'

And so from Italian casualties to our own. The body of Lieutenant Slaughter was never found; that of his pilot, Lieutenant Gerald Wentworth Loscombe Abingdon Bayly, was accorded the honourable treatment that one may expect from a civilized enemy. He lies now in the Military Cemetery at Bari. The other victim, L4A, was more fortunate. You will remember that we left Lieutenant-Commander Williamson in the water by the floating dock and Lieutenant Scarlett sitting there waiting upon events. Their captors behaved admirably towards their prey. 'In fact,' said Williamson, 'we were almost popular heroes. Two nights after our raid the RAF came over and we were put into an air-raid shelter full of seamen. They all pressed cigarettes on us and towards the end of the raid about twenty of them sang "Tipperary" for our benefit.' Scarlett was a more abrasive character. His obituarist observes that he 'was an excellent prisoner from the Allied point of view. He did much to annoy his captors and keep up the morale of his fellow POWs. In 1945 he was mentioned in despatches for organizing an attempt to escape from a camp near Lübeck.'

Everybody who had had any part in the business, fitter, rigger, aircrew and indeed all hands on both carriers, knew for certain that they had won a great and famous victory. Only one man seemed less persuaded. You will remember how, after Albuhera in 1811, Wellington came across General Beresford as he wrote 'a whining report that would have driven England mad'. The Duke found it necessary to explain to the other that he had won a great victory. Sir Andrew wrote no whining report but he never seemed quite to have taken in what his newest arm had achieved. The 'Manoeuvre well executed' signal may have been an ironic pleasantry, for the Navy well understands the value of meiosis.

But it was within the Admiral's power to mark the fact that it had been uncommonly well done by a fairly generous giving of decorations. When the immediate awards were announced the heavy displeasure of everybody concerned was soon made manifest. DSOs to the two flight leaders were natural enough, even though the absent Williamson would have to wait for his. The four DSCs went to Scarlett, to two other observers and to a pilot from *Eagle*. The entire company of *Illustrious* rose up in wrath at such a niggardly grant, the more so because not a single pilot from their ship, squadron commanders apart, received anything. Some unidentifiable sailor tore down the notice from the board. Being the honest man he was, Sir Andrew admitted years afterwards that he had undervalued both the feat itself and those who had performed it. Very possibly, with his traditional background, he shared the opinion of the great Duke that a man ought not to be especially rewarded for doing what he ought to have done.* The simmering anger boiled when the awards for Matapan – 'many DSOs and scores of DSCs', Charles Lamb called them – were announced. In May, 1941, Captain Boyd, late of *Illustrious*,

* The Admiral was not blamed. The lack of generosity came from Whitehall.

found a well-disposed MP who was willing to ask a Question. Two more DSOs, fourteen more DSCs and Mentions in Despatches for all those left out were added. By then twenty of the forty who had flown to Taranto were dead.

Others less intimately concerned seemed to have a better understanding of what had been achieved. Admiral Pound wrote of it to Admiral Cunningham: 'Just before the news of Taranto the Cabinet were rather down in the dumps; but Taranto had a most amazing effect on them.' One has to sympathize. There can have been little joy around the Downing Street table towards the end of 1940. For a time there were beaming smiles and mutual congratulations.

It was not quite the same in the opposing camp. Count Ciano, Mussolini's unfortunate son-in-law, left a diary, written up in his prison cell at Verona shortly before his relation by marriage had him shot. Ciano tells, under '12 November 1940', of 'a black day. The British, without warning, have attacked the Italian fleet at anchor in Taranto, and have sunk the dreadnought *Cavour* and seriously damaged the battleships *Littorio* and *Duilio*. These ships will remain out of the fight for many months. I thought I would find the Duce downhearted. Instead he took the blow quite well and does not, at the moment, seem to have fully realized its gravity.' In this, at least, he made common cause with Admiral Cunningham. The stiff upper lip phase did not endure; rage took its place.

The Regia Aeronautica (which Ciano says was always poking fun at the navy)* tended to avoid Alexandria whilst the Fleet was in residence. It was now ordered to seek instant vengeance. During the absence of Cunningham's ships the Italian pilots flew in during daylight hours, hit a destroyer without doing her much harm and scattered time bombs around the anchorage near to the floating dock. This could have been serious but it was no sort of spectacular revenge. On the morning of 12 November three of the big CANT flying-boats were sent in to do all the damage they could. It did not amount to much and all of them were shot down by Fulmars from *Illustrious* as she returned to port. From

* Admiral Ricciardi, for his part, was continually grumbling about the inadequate or misleading intelligence supplied by the flying-boat 'shadowers'.

Mussolini's point of view there was only one thing to be done and he turned to his master. Hitler and Goering had a score of their own to settle with the British after the thrashing their Luftwaffe had received from the RAF's Fighter Command. Once they had grasped the fact that the balance of sea power in the Mediterranean turned almost wholly upon the existence of a single ship the word went out from Berlin.

Send in the Stukas. Sink the *Illustrious*.

9

'THE FURIOUS GERMAN
COMES'

Thomas Babington Macaulay
The Battle of Naseby

Most dictionaries explain 'oxymoron' in some such fashion as 'a figure of speech by means of which contradictory terms are expressed so as to form a phrase or epithet, as "cruel kindness" '. Oxymoronic is the only fitting adjective for the victory at Taranto. It reduced, even if only for a matter of months, the menace to our convoys posed by the Italian battlefleet, essential ones to Malta and Alexandria along with wasted ones to Greece and Crete. Against that, it brought, or contributed to bringing, the German Air Force into the Mediterranean for the first time. The Luftwaffe may not have been technically all that superior to the Regia Aeronautica but it played far rougher.

It may well be true, as Lord Macaulay once asserted, that man can not die better than facing fearful odds for the ashes of his fathers and the temples of his gods. Facing them for the ashes of other people's fathers is not quite the same thing. For the fourth – very nearly for the fifth – time in this war men were about to be sent to die or be ignominiously captured and precious equipment to be given away to the enemy in the name of honour and in the course of a hopeless campaign. Honour had led the BEF from strong positions into the open so that Belgium might not be able to reproach us. We had, indeed, only come into the war lest we be accused of dishonouring a pledge to the Poles. Then had come a near-miss over Finland, the sacrifice of potentially excellent but still half-trained troops in Norway and now, in the absence of an Italian fleet of heavy ships that could have made the transit of troops to Greece impossible, it was all to be done again.

No country is ever highly regarded by others because it keeps its pledged word at any cost; few countries, in fact, do so. Public opinion in America was, however, also a factor to be taken into account. It was bad enough for young Englishmen to be packed off to fight and die in the Balkans but they were, as the Spartan inscription at Thermopylae puts it, 'obedient to her laws'. The young men of Australia and New Zealand were under no such obligation; but they went, and did not complain. The Italians had begun their invasion on 28 October, 1940. A RAF contingent of four Squadrons flew to Athens. A weak infantry brigade was despatched to Crete and, by degrees, something over 4,000 AA gunners, RAF ground crews and depot troops joined the others in and around Athens.

The Greek campaign concerns this narrative only for one reason. It had, by the time of Taranto or shortly afterwards, become plain that the task of beating down resistance in south-east Europe was beyond the powers of Italy alone. The German army must help out, and the German air service was part of that army. The Luftwaffe moved into Sicily and, for the first time, interested itself in the war of Cunningham and Wavell, particularly in HMS *Illustrious*.

By the end of the year 1940 the Italians had been dispossessed of their airfield at Trapani, and Stuka-Geschwader 3, about 100 Ju 87b dive-bombers fresh from France, had moved in. Their main weapon was the 500 kilogram bomb, something like four times the size of those carried by the Swordfish; experience had showed them very seldom failing to explode and to carry a destructive power greater by far than that of the biggest shell.

Admiral Cunningham was not excessively worried, for he had far more with which to occupy his mind than the outside chance of his floating aerodrome being lost. *Eagle*, it is true, had a flight deck so thin that 'it wobbled underfoot if one was misguided enough to jump up and down', as Charles Lamb explained. *Illustrious*, on the other hand, had hers made of 3-inch thick Wittkowitz steel, the best in the world. Whereas, with *Eagle*, 'one direct hit would have blown the old girl sky-high', *Illustrious* had metal fire-proof curtains that made the hangars into three separate fire-proof units. *Eagle*'s 'action station' for non-flying aviators was the ward-room bar – on the entirely sound principle that when doing nothing useful one might as well die glass in hand; in *Illustrious* the standing order was for them to close up in the hangar until stood down. The ward-room stanchions were of tubular steel as thick as street lampposts. It looked very impressive and as safe as any London tube station.

On 9 December, 1940, General Wavell began his offensive in the Western Desert. The 15-inch guns of the Fleet shelled Maktila and Sidi Barrani effectively enough, comfortable in the thought that no Littorios or Cavours were likely to dispute it with them. *Eagle* contributed a number of Swordfishes whose pilots rapidly acquired the new, to them, art of dive-bombing tanks. They became rather good at it. The Fleet Air Arm had already demonstrated that the Navy had at last some power of hitting back. Now it was the turn of the Army, and very well it was doing it.

Christmas came and went; 1941 began its horrible course. On 7 January the entire fleet set out again, in an operation called 'Excess', for the purpose of running convoys from either end of the sea to Malta and to Crete. When the convoys were safely away it was the Admiral's intention to harass whatever shipping might be found along the coast of Italy. Both Rear-Admiral Lyster and Captain Boyd had begged him not to bring *Illustrious* within range of the Stukas, whose presence in Sicily was well known. She could be of little use as a travelling fighter aerodrome, for wear and tear had reduced the Fulmars of her 806 Squadron to a mere half-dozen fit to take off. Sir Andrew took another view. The morale of the fleet was so high when *Illustrious* was in sight that he would not answer for the consequences if she were not. *Illustrious* must remain on station.

It all began soon after dawn, about 7.30, on 10 January, at a point 5 or 6 miles from Pantellaria. Michael Torrens-Spence, being the Senior Pilot in 819 Squadron, had been admitted to confidential intelligence reports that were not common knowledge among his juniors. The inner and outer anti-submarine patrols by the Swordfishes had been laid down in the flying programme for the day; the inner patrol, due to take off at 08.30 and return four hours later, would meet the big convoy they were escorting in the Skerki Channel – commonly called Bomb Alley – and tasks were assigned to the few serviceable Fulmars.

Charles Lamb, earmarked for the inner patrol, smoked his

after-breakfast cigarette on the quarter-deck below the overhang of the deck above. Torrens-Spence, due to go out of sight of the Fleet with the more distant flight, stood by his side as they watched a destroyer far astern travelling at top speed, apparently trying to catch up. As the two young officers admired the sight of a genuine ocean greyhound at full stretch she broke into two pieces. The fore part went down instantly, the stern remained, a floating tin box. It could only have been the result of a mine for no torpedo could have hit a ship travelling at 30 knots. The channel was supposed to have been swept, but there could never be certainty about such things.

Torrens-Spence observed that he hoped there were no more scudding about, 'because it's going to be difficult enough today without the additional hazard of mines'. Asked to explain what he meant, Torrens-Spence said, 'It's not the Italians I'm worried about, it's the bloody Germans. They are going to steal the show today. Didn't you know?'

It did not take Lamb long to realize that he was listening to a very worried man. Torrens-Spence explained that Hitler was coming to Mussolini's aid, that *Illustrious* was his main interest, that there was an entire *Fliegerkorps* in Sicily, 'and we are going to see them in action today and we shall be their target'. There were over 300 aircraft in a *Fliegerkorps*, he explained, and most of them were Stuka dive-bombers. Torrens-Spence, knowing the measure of his companion, spoke freely. There was no need for *Illustrious* to be there; her aircraft could perfectly well have covered their convoy with the ship out of range of the Stukas. He ended with: 'This is a day you will never forget. You can thank your lucky stars that you are flying this morning and not sitting in the hangar at action stations.'

Michael Torrens-Spence spoke true. Lamb took off at 08.30 on his submarine hunt: nothing in particular happened and at 12.30 he waited over *Illustrious*' port quarter as she turned into the wind. Then, before he had done other than the routine drills before landing and was turning gently in with arrester-hook down, it all happened. There came a tremendous roar, clouds of smoke covered everything and every gun in the ship opened up. The next few moments were purest horror. Lamb saw a strange aircraft flying across his bows, a huge red swastika painted on the side of its grey fuselage. A single burst from his Vickers gun hit nothing; the Stuka 'dipped as though in salute and dropped an enormous great bomb right down the after lift-well, which was still gaping. The bomb looked like a GPO pillar box painted black. By the flames which shot out through the hole in the deck I realized that it had exploded in the hangar. Then the lift itself burst out of the deck and shot a few feet into the air and sank back into the lift-well on its side, like a great wedge-shaped hunk of cheese.' Hardly had he taken in the horror of what had happened than Lamb was stunting for his life, along with his air-gunner, in a battle where the Swordfish was hopelessly outclassed.

The JU 87b was a modern, all-metal monoplane with a range of just under 500 miles, a maximum speed of 242 mph, a ceiling of 28,000 feet and a rate of climb of 1500 feet a minute. A complicated arrangement of diving brakes enabled it, monoplane that it was, to dive and return at a velocity that would have torn a Stringbag to pieces. Add to that two fixed machine guns in the wings and a moveable one in the stern and you have a machine tailor-made for ship-smashing. In a dog-fight the Swordfish would have no more chance of shooting one down than a hansom-cab of racing a taxi. The best that the pilot could hope for was that by pressing Stringbag's manoeuvrability almost to destruction he might come out alive. This, possible only to a pilot of exceptional skill and experience, was what Charles Lamb succeeded in doing. As he put it, 'The Stukas must have thought that they were attacking some weird kind of hovering flying bedstead which could spin round within its own wing-span.'* Lamb and his crew survived; there was no *Illustrious* on which to land but he was able to ditch his riddled machine hard by a destroyer. Torrens-Spence had not exaggerated. Even these experiences were better by far than the ones endured aboard the target ship.

Whether by clever scheming or mere accident will never now be known, but the Fulmars which alone might have coped with at least some of the Stukas had been drawn off. At almost exactly

---

* It is a Fleet Air Arm Article of Faith that no Stuka was capable of shooting down the agile Swordfish, nor did one ever perform the feat. Another pilot, Lamb's contemporary, tells me that 'I always believed that Lamb was shot down by a Me 109 or a Heinkel . . . If he was shot down by a Stuka I think he must have been having an off day.'

12.30, as Lamb was making ready to land, two Italian torpedo-bombers came in low and let drive at *Valiant*. These were the immediate cause of the outburst of fire from *Illustrious* but, though their torpedoes missed, they started the rot. The Fulmars, patrolling high above the Fleet, spotted them and dived to the rescue. Admiral Cunningham watched it all.

At precisely the moment that they had lost more height than could be recovered in time, 'large formations of aircraft were sighted to the northward, and were very soon overhead. They were recognized as German, three squadrons of Stukas. The *Illustrious* flew off more fighters but neither they nor the patrol already in the air could gain sufficient height to do anything. We opened up with every AA gun we had as one by one the Stukas peeled into their dives, concentrating the whole venom of their attack upon the *Illustrious*. At times she became almost completely hidden in a forest of great bomb splashes. One was too interested in this new form of dive-bombing attack really to be frightened, and there was no doubt that we were watching complete experts. Formed roughly in a large circle over the fleet they peeled off one by one on reaching the attacking position. We could not but admire the skill and precision of it all. The attacks were pressed home to point-blank range, and as they pulled out of their dives some of them were seen to fly along the flight deck of the *Illustrious* below the level of her funnel.'

Admiral Cunningham saw much from the bridge of his flagship but he could have had little enough idea of what was happening inside his only modern ship. 'I saw her hit early on just before the bridge and in all, in something like 10 minutes, she was hit by six 1,000-lb bombs, to leave the line badly on fire, her steering gear crippled, her lifts out of action, and with heavy casualties.' Sir Andrew's gift of understatement was always marked. 'To leave the line' is a proper and dignified turn of phrase, of the kind used often enough by Rodney or Jervis. It hardly conveys the stark horror of the slaughter house that *Illustrious'* interior had become.

The Luftwaffe, being a land animal, had no use for or understanding of torpedoes. To Goering, Milch and the rest of their tribe the bomb was the thing and the bigger the bomb the better. It was quite possible for anyone in the target area to watch while the single great cylinder was swung down into position between

131

the wheels where it remained on view for a couple of seconds before falling. Given time, the watcher on the ground could learn how best to avoid being blasted to atoms and how to hit back. *Illustrious* had no time. The Stukas began their pull-out at something like 5,000 feet, having built up a terrific speed in the dive from 10,000, and released the bomb, still diving, at about 500. Once the bomb had been released the bomber followed after it and the accuracy obtained was something the Navy had not experienced outside Norwegian waters.

The first bomb of them all, the one Lamb had seen, did most of the damage. Half a ton of steel and explosive, neatly shot down the after lift, had exploded in the hangar; the blast effect was, from the German point of view, exactly what was needed, right under the flight deck. The fine thick armour might as well have been made of linoleum for all the protection it afforded. The forward lift, all 300 tons of it, was bent into a hoop. The thick stanchions of the ward room were twisted like ornamental candles, though the clock continued to tick away. An officer of the RAF, there as an observer and with no particular duties, very sensibly sat himself down in an armchair, tried to ignore the hellish noise and read *The Times*. He was found later with the paper still in his hands; it was his head that was missing.

The worst place to be was in the hangar, the concentrated mass of everything that was most combustible and explosive in the entire ship; it was, however, the action station of all aircrews not engaged in flying and presence there cost the Taranto crews a great deal. As bomb after bomb fell, near-misses bending the keel and damaging the steering, three direct hits went straight through the flight deck and the hangar deck also before bursting in the wardroom beneath.

In the great smoke-filled butcher's shop the casualties mounted. Lieutenant Clifford, pilot of the late-starting L5F who had watched his own bombs fail to explode over the Mar Piccolo, was 'last seen severely wounded by bomb splinters and is believed to have been blown overboard during one of the many attacks'.

His observer, Going, was a little more fortunate. 'During continuous German dive-bombing attacks Lieutenant Going was working below with damage control parties when he had a leg blown off by a bomb which wrecked the carrier's steering compartment.'

Much of this was caused by the fire-screens which, says Lamb, 'disintegrated at once, bursting apart in masses of red-hot steel splinters about 3 or 4 feet long, which tore through every obstruction setting on fire all the aircraft that were not already burning and decapitating anyone who might be standing in the way.' One of these was Lieutenant Neil Kemp, whose torpedo from L4K had bagged *Littorio*. The official report merely says that 'He was killed when a 1,000-lb bomb penetrated the deck of *Illustrious* and exploded in the hangar'.

Lamb, who was told all about it soon enough, expanded: 'He [Kemp] had been standing in front of Jackie Jago when the first sudden explosion occurred. Jackie found himself facing a headless body, which was all that was left of a fine chap who would have made a wonderful admiral had he lived. Even in death Neil refused to lie down until Jackie gave his grim remains a little push.'

The RNVR element was badly cut up. Out of four officers only one survived the bombing. Anthony Francis Xavier Mardel-Ferreira was killed outright; Edgar Perkins 'was knocked unconscious during the German dive bombing attacks. Whilst lying unconscious in the wardroom he was drowned by subsequent flooding.' The last of the young VR sub-lieutenants, Anthony Leonard Osterfield Wray, 'succumbed to wounds received during the attack by German dive-bomers' and died on the following day. Lieutenant Skelton, pilot of L5B, and Lieutenant Perkins, who had been his observer, both died of wounds during the bombing or shortly afterwards. Morford, pilot of the unlucky L5Q which had lost its petrol tank on the way to Taranto, had almost reason to envy them. He 'was very badly burned when *Illustrious* was attacked. . . . He survived, and after extensive plastic surgery continued serving until 1947.' Going also returned to duty, minus one leg, and remained there until the same year. Six of the aircrews, four of them pilots, were dead; it should have been a satisfactory revenge. The total of the casualties was eight-three killed and sixty-odd seriously wounded.

One of the German officers, Lieutenant-Colonel Hozzell, told Lamb after the war that a second strike had been planned but the Luftwaffe ran out of bombs and the weather worsened. There is no reason to disbelieve him, nor to doubt his conviction about leaving *Illustrious* 'lop-sided, unremoveable, protected by four destroyers'. Lop-sided she was, but not unremoveable. By some high-class seamanship and superhuman efforts from all hands Captain Boyd got her at 26 knots to Malta where once more the Stukas set about the battered ship. This time they would not have it all their own way, not with Fulmars flying from the island bases, along with the Hurricanes of the RAF.

Illustrious' Swordfish pilots were not to be completely left out. Sparke, of L4C who had followed Williamson and Scarlett over San Pietro, turned fighter pilot for the last four months of his life. As the Fulmars fought their battles throughout the almost hourly bombings in Valletta Harbour, Sparke was converted to the Sea Hurricane and struck back. He died, as he would probably have wished, ramming a German bomber.

Illustrious was a fortnight in Malta, alongside Parlatario Wharf and under something like constant attack. Two more bombs hit her, three near-misses lifted her out of the water and damaged her hull. The engineers worked as men can seldom have worked before, among the unimagineable beastliness left uncleaned up, and on 24 January, 1941, she left under her own steam, first to Alexandria and then on to the United States for repairs lasting a full year. Vickers Armstrong at Barrow-in-Furness had built her honestly and well; it was hardly their fault that the power of dive-bombing was not understood.

Admiral Cunningham had cause for worry. He had seen the whole balance of naval power changed for the worse at one blow and was persuaded that 'The efforts of the Regia Aeronautica were almost as nothing compared with those of these deadly Stukas of the Luftwaffe'. That there was no denying. Mitchell had been right after all.

This was the quintessence of the Mitchell idea; no torpedoes but huge bombs, delivered not in salvoes but one at a time, each carefully aimed at a specific part of the ship. *Illustrious*, however, was no moored hulk and the fight her gunners put up probably saved her. There was no other help at hand. It is profitless, though tempting, to wonder what difference a dozen Oerlikons and a few Bofors might have made.

I O

REVENGE, ITALIAN STYLE

The Royal Navy, having not suffered all that number of defeats in its long history, has always been properly sporting in its attitude to those who have, for the moment, got the better of it. The pilots of the Stukas were not loved, but they were respected and admired for professional skill and courage. It was, however, never quite so generous to the other enemy of this period. The furious German, as might be expected, came not with his trumpets and his drums but with the thunder and the lightnings of *Götterdämmerung*, the Ride of the Valkyries and all the other loud noises of the Führer's favourite composer. Not so the Italians. They had in their store of accumulated knowledge ways of destroying battleships with far less dramatic effect. The stiletto is not as showy as the morgenstern but quite as effective.

The first demonstration of its use for nearly 23 years came on a spring morning off the coast of Crete. HMS *York*, Sir Andrew's only 8-inch gunned cruiser, lay peacefully at anchor in Suda Bay as Italian ships had done in the Mar Grande. From nowhere in particular there emerged, at top speed, six tiny objects, some heading for *York* and others for the tanker *Pericles*. The successors to Luigi Rizzo had arrived. Before anything could be done about it all of them had exploded up against their targets. *York* was flooded and had to be beached; *Pericles* was holed, but her cargo salvaged. It was a notable naval victory with no loss of life. Six Italians were picked up from rafts, quite willing to explain that they and their infernal machines had been brought by torpedo-boat and turned loose as soon as they were within range. It was an exhibition of coolness and bravery deserving of the highest praise. It did not get it, for the Navy, though properly sensible of the courage the Italians had shown, was outraged. Gentlemen who called themselves seamen did not make war in this fashion. It was worse than shooting foxes; more like poisoning them.

Vice-Admiral Baillie-Grohman, when he came to write his book ten years later, was still choleric enough to have a picture of *York* sitting on the bottom captioned as 'Holed by Italian Desperadoes'. He did not mean it as a compliment. Certainly a feat so despicable had no lessons for a great and ancient sea power. Attila was a worthier enemy than a Borgia.

Time went by and the regrettable incident came to be forgotten. Ten days after Peal Harbor – of which more later – the great and ancient battleships were at Alexandria. At the harbour mouth were a boom and net defences; around each ship were more nets. The disposition of the Fleet was, in fact, very much like that of the Italians in the harbour of Taranto a little over a year earlier. As then, attack from the air was very much a possibility and every proper precaution against it had been taken.

There was no attack from the air. Instead the Admiral was awakened from sleep in his cabin aboard *Queen Elizabeth* with the news that a couple of Italians had been found clinging to *Valiant*'s bow buoy. As they had had nothing to the point to tell their interrogators they had been sent ashore under arrest. The Admiral had a longer memory. On his orders the men were brought back to *Valiant* and made comfortable in a forward compartment below the waterline. That was at about 04.00. Sir Andrew put his ships' companies to work rowing guard boats around and dropping small charges while others were made to drag chains along their ships' bottoms. The Italians remained enigmatic. Just before 06.00 came the first explosion, badly damaging a tanker and a destroyer. Twenty minutes later there erupted a heavier one under *Valiant* and four minutes after that one under the flagship. Both *Valiant* and *Queen Elizabeth* were quickly reduced to what Mr Churchill called 'a useless burden for months'. It had not been glorious but at least the Admiral was spared the fate of Captain von Vukovic.

Praise, though stinted, was undoubtedly due. The two men who had fixed the charge to the propellors of the tanker changed out of their diving suits, walked ashore and had the misfortune to be arrested. The pair incarcerated in *Valiant* decided that when the explosion was nearly due they might as well tell the Captain. At this point they took him into their confidence. The intensity of the cold, after hours in the water, had made them unable to fix their mine to *Valiant*'s hull as they had intended. The best they had been able to do was drop it to some point on the harbour bottom about 15 feet below her keel. For good measure, as became kinsmen of the Borgias, they had also scattered tins of calcium carbide broadcast in order to touch off the fuel oil that must inevitably gush out after the explosion. Shortly afterwards the explosion followed. Positioning may have been less than perfect but the charge blew *Valiant* out of the water. The Italian *'fecero saltare'* sounds far more descriptive. 'Make to jump'. She, too, would be *hors de combat* for a long time.

The two paladins who had attended to *Queen Elizabeth* had better fortune, though still less than they deserved. Having put their horrible machine in place they swam ashore, changed into plain clothes and tried to finish the plan for a rendezvous with their submarine. Fate got in first. To begin with they incurred suspicion by trying to get change for a £5 note, by no means the commonest of currencies. That done, though regarded with some suspicion, they booked into an hotel at Rosetta where they enjoyed, one may hope, a refreshing night's sleep. In the morning they sought for their accomplices but found none. Being thus abandoned, they enquired about a train for Cairo where a well-disposed brother Latin, the Spanish Consul, might be expected to take care of them. Luck, however, had run out and the adventurers underwent the fate that Bismarck had predicted for any British army that might land in Pomerania. Somebody called a policeman.

Revenge for Taranto seemed almost poetic. But the war had run barely a quarter of its course and soon even these things would seem to have come out of an earlier world. Not all of the aircrews would live to see it, for long life is not guaranteed to those who make up the British armed forces early in the country's wars. The two young Sub-Lieutenants Bailey and Macaulay, as mentioned earlier, died when tearing the wings off their Stringbag. John Buscall, last of the RNVR officers present, was killed soon afterwards, flying from the FAA airfield by Alexandria. Hale's observer, Lieutenant G.A. Carline, was killed in December, 1941, when the carrier *Audacity* was torpedoed by a submarine, R.W.V. Hamilton was shot down and killed during an attack on Leros, and Sub-Lieutenant J.R.B. Weekes shared the same fate. Lieutenant M.R. Maund was 'killed whilst flying on anti-shipping operations from Malta with 828 Squadron'. Julian Sparke, who transferred to the fighters after *Illustrious* had been bombed, had four more months of life left to him. When attacking a formation of German aircraft from *Formidable* – successor to *Illustrious* – he rammed one and died with it. The post-war Taranto dinners held nothing like a full muster.

No opportunity came to the Royal Navy of carrying out such an operation again, but it had demonstrated what could be done against the seemingly impregnable battle fleets by forces almost insignificant in size and power. How much more could be done on a far larger scale would be demonstrated before 1941 was out, a long way from the Mediterranean. It was still the new men, the young men of the Fleet Air Arm in their almost comical aircraft and with their non-explosive bombs who had set the stage and introduced the characters for the next performance. At Pearl Harbor.

APPENDIX I

Some particulars of the Fairey Swordfish

Origin	Prototype appeared in 1934, as replacement for the Baffin. Designed as 2–3 seater Fleet torpedo-spotter-reconnaissance aircraft. Reached TSR Squadrons on carriers 1937.
Power Plant	One Bristol Pegasus III M3 motor. Maximum power 750 hp at 4750 feet at 2525 rpm. Cruising 680 hp at 2200 rpm at 3,500 feet. Take-off 775 hp.
Construction	Wings – 2 steel spars. Main ribs steel; secondary duralumin. Fabric covered. Tail unit – metal frame, fabric covered. Undercarriage – wheels interchangeable with floats. An inflatable dinghy was housed in the port wing.
Dimensions	Span 45 ft 6 ins. Length (landplane) 36 ft 4 ins. Length (floatplane) 40 ft 11 ins. Height (landplane) 12 ft 10 ins. Height (floatplane) 14 ft 7 ins.
Area	Wings 542 sq ft.
Weights	Empty (landplane), 4, 195 lbs. Loaded, 7,720 lbs. Disposable, 3,525 lbs.

Performance   (Landplane). Maximum speed 154 mph at
                   7,000 ft. Cruising, 131 mph at 3,500 ft. Sea-
                   level 141 mph. Landing 63 mph. Initial climb,
                   1220 ft/min. Service ceiling, 19,250 ft.
                   Absolute ceiling, 21,000 ft. Duration 5.7 hrs.
                   Range 750 miles.

Loadings   Wings 14.33 lbs/sq ft. Power 9.9 lb/hp.

Taken from *Aircraft of the Fighting Powers*, 1940 edition.

APPENDIX II

Fleet Air Arm Officers who took part in the Taranto Raid but did not survive the Second World War

Killed in the bombing of HMS *Illustrious*, January, 1941

Lieutenant E.W. Clifford, DSO, RN
Lieutenant N.McI. Kemp, DSC, RN
Sub-Lieutenant (A) A.F.X. Mardel-Ferreira, RNVR
Sub-Lieutenant (A) E.A. Perkins, RNVR
Lieutenant (A) R.G. Skelton, RN
Sub-Lieutenant (A) A.L.O. Wray, RNVR

Killed in subsequent operations

Sub-Lieutenant (A) R.A. Bailey, DSC, RN
Sub-Lieutenant (A) J. Buscall, RNVR
Lieutenant G.A. Carline, DSC, RN
Lieutenant R.W.V. Hamilton, DSC, RN
Lieutenant P.N. Humphreys, GC, RN*

---

* 'On 13 May, 1937, the destroyer HMS *Hunter* was mined off Almeria on the coast of Spain. The mine exploded under the Petty Officer Stokers' and Torpedomen's Mess Decks. The ship was believed to be in imminent danger of sinking but Humphreys and a Petty Officer, James Smail, jumped down 8 feet into oil fuel on to a partly destroyed deck. The ladder had been blown away. They spent some ten minutes dragging living and dead men from out of the wreckage and the oil, passing them up to those on deck. The citation states that the rescued had all swallowed oil and would have died if left; others were wounded and their immersion in the oil, if prolonged, would undoubtedly have caused their deaths.' Petty Officer Smail also received the EGM; five other Petty Officers and Leading Seamen were decorated for the same incident. *London Gazette*, 12 November, 1937.

(continued over)

Sub-Lieutenant (A) A.S.D. Macaulay, DSC, RN
Lieutenant M.R. Maund, RN
Sub-Lieutenant (A) P.D.J. Sparke, DSC, RN
Sub-Lieutenant (A) J.R.B. Weekes, DSC, RN

In 1940 the Empire Gallantry Medal was converted to the George Cross.

Lumley St George Lyster, Rear-Admiral at the time of Taranto, left the Service with the rank of Admiral in 1945, having served as Fifth Sea Lord and Chief of Naval Air Services, and finally as Flag Officer Carrier Training. In 1917, along with two other officers of the same rank, Lieutenant-Commander Lyster had been decorated with the Order of the Crown of Italy. His award appears in the *London Gazette* for 12 May of that year; at almost exactly the same time the Order was conferred on Luigi Rizzo who himself achieved Flag rank in 1936 as Il Conte di Grado. What were Lyster's services I am unable to say. The Italian authorities plead shortage of staff for such research. The Admiralty Library in Whitehall, to which I was referred by the Archivist of the Royal Naval College, Greenwich, has answered neither of my letters on the subject.

APPENDIX III

A Brief Comparison of Taranto with Pearl Harbor

The day that 'will live in infamy' was a Sunday, in time of peace. The first wave of Japanese aircraft, forty torpedo bombers, forty-nine high-level bombers, fifty-nine dive-bombers and the same number of fighters swarmed over the coastline and broke formation. The fighters flew off to destroy the parked US aircraft, the high-level bombers to destroy those parked on Hickam Field, adjoining the Navy Yard, while the dive-bombers went for the battleships. The first attack lasted about half an hour, from 07.55 to 08.25; it caused something like 90 per cent of the damage. Sixteen torpedo-bombers, coming in low above the water, went for the sleeping battleships, *Arizona* on her own and the other four in pairs.

At the same time dive-bombers, some carrying converted 16-inch armour-piercing shells, added their contribution. Then came a lull for about a quarter of an hour before the second striking force came in: fifty high-level and eighty dive-bombers, accompanied by forty fighters. This time the Americans were better ready for them and far less damage was done. Again it was ground fire versus aircraft, for no chance of fighter intervention existed. In two hours the US Navy had lost 2,000 killed and 710 wounded – thrice, as Morison points out, the entire casualty list of its last two wars put together. Seven battleships had been sunk or badly damaged, along with three destroyers and about half the aircraft on the island.

For all the devastation and murder it had managed, the Imperial Japanese Navy had lost not a battle but the war. The battleships, as the Royal Navy had learnt, did not matter all that much in the long run. What did matter was that the carrier fleet remained in being and it was to be the carriers that, in good time, would break the Japanese Navy. The message was not believed. For years the great powers went on building battleships. They looked so terribly impressive.

In a little over a year Taranto had become almost ancient history. Once the attack on Pearl Harbor was over and the *Prince of Wales* and *Repulse* had been sunk in the fashion prophesied by Sir Arthur Harris mastery of the seas passed across the Atlantic. But it was still the lightly-regarded Italian Navy that had notched up the highest score at the lowest cost.

BIBLIOGRAPHY

Printed Books

WHISPERS FROM THE FLEET, Rear-Admiral Sir Christopher Cradock, Gieves 1908

A NAVAL LIEUTENANT 1914–1918, Stephen King-Hall ('Etienne'), Methuen 1919

THE AMERICAN FLYING BOAT, Capt. R.C. Knott, USN. US Naval Institute, Annapolis, 1979

THE LIFE & LETTERS OF DAVID, LORD BEATTY, Ed. Rear-Admiral W.S. Chalmers, Hodder & Stoughton 1951

A SAILOR'S ODYSSEY, Admiral of the Fleet Lord Cunningham of Hyndhope, Hutchinson 1951

THOUGHTS & ADVENTURES, W.S. CHURCHILL, Odhams 1932

STEP BY STEP, W.S. CHURCHILL, Odhams 1939

THE UNRELENTING STRUGGLE (Speeches), W.S. CHURCHILL, Cassell 1942

THE MEMOIRS OF LORD ISMAY, Heinemann 1960

ONE MARINE'S TALE, Major-General Sir Leslie Hollis, Andre Deutsch, 1956

BRITANNIA AT DARTMOUTH, S.W.C. Pack, Alvin Redman 1966

WINGED WARFARE, E.J. Kingston McCloughry, Cape 1937

THE STRATEGY OF SEA POWER, S.W. Roskill, Collins 1962

NAVAL POLICY BETWEEN THE WARS, S.W. Roskill, Collins 1968

THE BLUNTED SWORD, David Divine, Hutchinson 1964

PER ARDUA, Hilary St George Saunders, OUP 1944

VICKERS: A HISTORY, J.D. Scott, Weidenfeld & Nicolson 1962

FIGHTS AND FLIGHTS, C.R. Samson, Benn 1930

NAVAL OPERATIONS (1914–1918) Vols IV & V, Sir Julian Corbett, Longmans 1920

THE WAR IN THE AIR (6 VOLS), Sir Walter Raleigh & H.A. Jones, 1922–1937
NAVAL STAFF HISTORY, Second World War, BR 1736 (6)
THE NORWEGIAN CAMPAIGN OF 1940, J.L. Moulton, Eyre & Spottiswoode, 1966
GREEK TRAGEDY '41, Anthony Heckstall-Smith & Rear-Admiral H.T. Baillie-Grohman, Blond 1961
WAR IN A STRINGBAG, Charles Lamb, Cassell 1977
THE MEN'S END: SWORDFISH 1941, Lindsay Houston, The Book Guild 1986
WITH NAVAL WINGS, John Wellham, Staplemount 1995
THE FLEET AIR ARM, Reginald Longstaff, Hale 1981
THE FOUR ARK ROYALS, Michael Apps, William Kimber 1976
AIRCRAFT OF THE FIGHTING POWERS, 1940, Harborough 1941
ANTIQUES OF THE AIR, Michael F. Jerram, New English Library ND

The Files of *The Daily Telegraph*
Seedie's Fleet Air Arm List, various dates.

From Italian Sources
LA MARINA ITALIANA NELLA SECONDA GUERRA MONDIALE, Vol IV
'LE AZIONI NAVALE IN MEDITERRANEO DEL GIUGNO 1940 AL MARZO 1941'
   'Ufficio Storico Della Marina Militare, Roma 1976'
I MEZZI D'ASSALTO (on the Bomba Bay action and the attack on HMSs Valiant and Queen Elizabeth) Caps II and IX
ATTACCO CONTRO LA FLOTTA NELLA BASE DI TARANTO (Notte sul 12 Novembre 1940)
NOTO BIOGRAFICHE DI LUIGI RIZZO
MED D'ORO RAFFAELLE ROSSETTI

On Pearl Harbor
THE HISTORY OF UNITED STATES NAVAL OPERATIONS IN WORLD WAR II, Samuel Eliot Morison
BATTLESHIP ARIZONA: An Illustrated History, Paul Stillwell

INDEX

As nearly all the officers named were of the Royal Navy the suffix RN has been omitted. As have Orders and decorations. Ranks are those held at the time.

A

Asquith, The Rt. Hon. H.H., 22

B

Babington, Sub-Lieut. J.H., RNAS, 19
Bailey, Sub-Lieut. (A) R.A., 55, 91, 104, 137, 141
Baille-Grohman, Vice Admiral H.T., 136
Balbo, Marshal Italo, 33
Balfour, The Rt. Hon. A.J., 13, 39
Barnacle, Bandmaster Percy, 31
Bayly, Lieut. G.W.L.A., 93, 110, 115, 122
'Bartimaeus', see Ritchie, Capt. Sir L.
Beatty, Admiral Sir David, 22, 24, 27
Beaumont, Colonel F., 3
Billing, Noel Pemberton, 19
Bolt, Rear Admiral A.S., 63–4
Bootham, Flight-Lieut. J.N., RAF, 47
Bowker, Midshipman J., 91, 107

Boyd, Capt. D.W., 85, 122–3, 134
Briggs, Squadron Cmdr. E.F., RNAS, 19, 20
Bull, Sub-Lieut. W.A., 91, 104
Buscall Sub-Lieut. (A)., J. RNVR, 92, 104, 137, 141

C

Cannon, Flight Sub-Lieut. R.P., RNAS, 19
Carline, Lieut. G.A., 93, 110, 138, 141
Carson, The Rt. Hon. Sir Edward, 22
Chalmers, Rear Admiral W.S., 43
Childers, Erskine, 19, 20
Churchill, The Rt. Hon. W.S., 9, 10, 12, 27, 30, 39, 40, 42, 76, 118–19, 136
Ciano, Count Galeazzo, 124
Clifford, Lieut. E.W., 94, 109, 113, 132
Cochrane, Admiral Sir T. (Lord Dundonald), 30
Cradock, Rear Admiral Sir Christopher, 8

Cunningham, Admiral Sir
Andrew, 41, 66, 70–8, 80–1,
85–6, 113–14, 123, 127–8,
134, 136
Curtiss, Glenn H., 15

D

Dacre, Flight Lieut. G.B., RNAS,
13
Dorling, Capt. H. Taprell, 7, 41
Douhet, General, 36
Dunning, Squadron Cmdr. E.H.,
RNAS, 24

E

Eden, The Rt. Hon. Anthony, 76
Edmonds, Flight Cmdr. C.K.,
RNAS, 13
Ely, Eugene, 10

F

Fairey, C.R., 47
Fisher, Admiral Sir J., 11, 13
Fisher, Admiral Sir W.W., 58
Forde, Sub-Lieut. (A) A.J., 92,
107
Franco, General Francisco, 79, 80

G

Gazda, Antoine, 54
Godefroy, Admiral (Fr.), 71
Going, Lieut. G.R.M., 95, 108–9,
113, 132
Goodwin, Lieut. D.G., 92, 106
Gray, Cmdr. Spencer, RNAS, 11
Green, Sub-Lieut. R.A.F., 95, 109
Grey, Capt. Andrew, 32
Grieve, Lieut. K.C., 92, 101, 105,
108
Grumman, Leroy, 38, 50
Guidoni, Captain A., 2, 3, 11

H

Hale, Lieut.-Cmdr., J.W., 93,
110, 137
Hamel, Gustav, 11
Hamilton, Lieut. R.W.V., 94,
110, 141
Harris, Group Captain Arthur,
RAF, 40
Hawker, H.G., 11
Hollis, Maj.-Gen. L.C., RM, 40
Holmes, Professor, 8
Houston, Lieut. Lindsay, RNVR,
50
Hozzell, Lieut.Col. (Luftwaffe),
133
Humphreys, Lieut. P., 94, 12,
141

I

Ismay, Major-General Hastings,
76

J

Jackson, Admiral Sir H., 13
Janvrin, Lieut. H.R.B., 92, 101,
108, 116
Jellicoe, Admiral Sir John, 14, 21
Jones, Sub-Lieut. (A) P.D., 93,
110,112–13

K

Keighley-Peach, Cmdr. C.L., 32,
74–5
Kemp, Lieut. N. mcI., 91, 104,
107, 115, 119, 132
Kerr, Rear Admiral Mark, 17
Kiggell, Lieut L.J., 64, 91, 99,
101–8, 116
King, Admiral Ernest J., USN, 38

L

Lamb, Lieut. (A) C.B., 51, 64, 91, 99, 101–8,113–16, 123, 127–30
Lea, Lieut. (A) C.S.G., 93, 110–13, 120
Lewis, Capt. Roger, 67
Lobelle, Marcel, 48
Longmore, Sir Arthur, 18, 41, 59, 76, 81
Lyster, Lieut.-Cmdr. (later Rear Admiral) L. St. G., 18, 41, 58, 81, 98, 128

M

Macaulay, Sub-Lieut. (A) A.S.D., 55, 92, 101–13, 137, 141
Mardel-Ferreira, Sub-Lieut. (A) A.F.X., RNVR, 92, 107, 132
Marix, Squadron Cmdr. R.G., RNAS, 11
Maund, Lieut. M.R., 91, 104, 138, 141
Mitchell, R.J., (mtd.), 43, 47
Mitchell, Cmdr. Sir Steuart, 54
Mitchell, Brig.-Gen W., USA, 37, 134
Moffett, Rear Admiral W.R., USN, 38
Morford, Lieut. (A) A.W.D., 95, 109, 132
Mountbatten, Lord Louis, 54
Murray, Lieut. (A) J.B., 92, 107
Mussolini, Benito, 33, 57, 98, 125

N

Neale, Sub-Lieut. (A) A.L.O., 92, 101
Northcliffe, Lord, 15

P

Paine, Sub-Lieut. (A) S.M., 92, 107
Pakenham, Admiral Sir W., 30
Paolucci, Tenente Raffaele, 35
Patch, Capt. O., RM, 75, 92, 106
Perkins, Sub-Lieut. (A) E.A., 94, 110, 132
Phillips, Admiral Sir Tom, 40–1
Poag, Professor C. Wylie, 99
Porte, Cmdr. J.C., 14–16
Pound, Admiral Sir Dudley, 65, 70, 124
Pridham-Wippell, Vice Admiral H.D., 86
Prothero, Capt. R.C. ('Prothero the Bad'), 81
Pugliese, Engineer Inspector-General U., 120

R

Rawlinson, Lieut.-Col. A., 14
Riccardi, Admiral, 71–2, 114
Ritchie (formerly Ricci), Capt. Sir L., 7, 13, 27, 41
Rizzo, Capitano Luigi, 34, 135
Ross, Lieut. George, 39, 54
Rossetti, Maggiore Raffaele, 35

S

Samson, Cmdr. C.R., RNAS, 9, 12
Sarra, Sub-Lieut. (A) W.C., 92, 107
Scarlett, (later Scarlett-Streatfeild), Lieut. N., 91, 98, 101 et seq., 122–3
Scott, Admiral Sir Percy, 9
Short Bros., 9
Sippe, Flight Lieut. S.V., RNAS, 19, 20

Skelton, Lieut. (A) R.G., 94, 110, 132

Slaughter, Lieut. H.J., 93, 110, 122

Smuts, General J.C., 26

Somerville, Admiral Sir James, 41, 80

Sopwith, T.O.M., 9, 14

Sparke, Sub-Lieut. (A) P.D.J., 92, 101, 103, 111, 134, 138, 141

Stainforth, Flight-Lieut. G.H, RAF, 47

Sueter, Capt. Murray, 9, 12, 14, 18

Summers, Capt. Joseph ('Mutt'), 40–4, 48

Sutton, Lieut. A.W.F., 94

Swayne, Lieut. (A) H.A.I., 92, 100, 104, 116, 119

T

'Taffrail', see Dorling, Capt. H.T.

Tegetthoff, Baron Wilhelm von (mtd.) 34

Thursby, Rear Admiral C.F., 17

Torrens-Spence, Lieut. F.M.A., 76, 94, 110–15, 119, 128, 130

Tovey, Vice Admiral John, 69, 75

Trenchard, Maj.-Gen. Sir H., 23

V

Von Voukovic, Captain, 36

W

Wanamaker, Rodman, 15

Waring, Air Commodore, E.F., 16

Wavell, General Sir Archibald, 76, 128

Weekes, Sub-Lieut. (A) J.R.B., 94, 110, 138, 141

Wellham, Lieut. (A) J.W.G., 50, 84, 89, 93, 111–12, 121

Welsh, Flight Lieut. W.L., RNAS, 21

Whittle, Flight Lieut. F., RAF, 48

Williamson, Lieut.-Cmdr. K., 90, 98, 101 et seq., 120–3

Wray, Sub-Lieut. (A) A.L.O., RNVR, 92, 101, 132

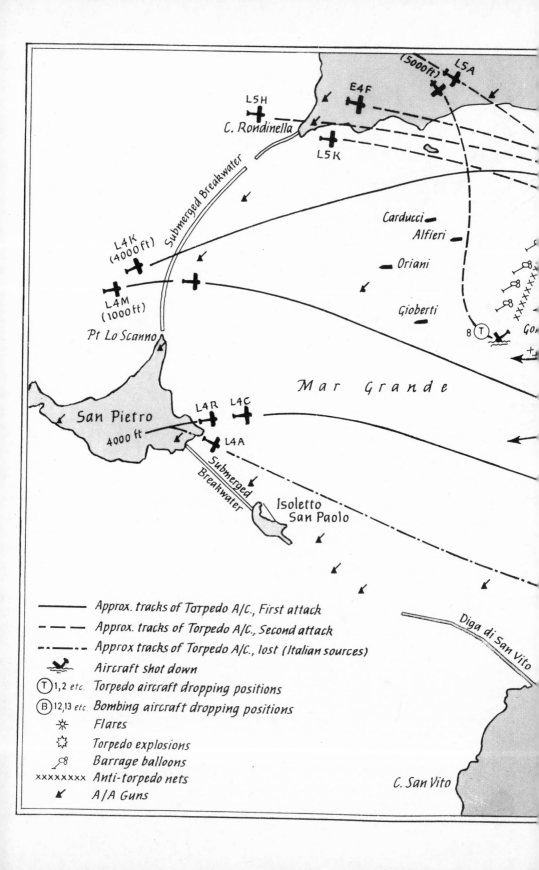

L5A (5000 ft)

E4F

L5H

C. Rondinella

L5K

Submerged Breakwater

L4K (4000 ft)

L4M (1000 ft)

Pt Lo Scanno

Carducci

Alfieri

Oriani

Gioberti

8 (T)

Go

Mar Grande

San Pietro

4000 ft

L4R   L4C

L4A

Submerged Breakwater

Isoletto San Paolo

Diga di San Vito

—————— Approx. tracks of Torpedo A/C., First attack

– – – – – Approx. tracks of Torpedo A/C., Second attack

–·–·–·– Approx tracks of Torpedo A/C., lost (Italian sources)

Aircraft shot down

(T) 1,2 etc. Torpedo aircraft dropping positions

(B) 12,13 etc. Bombing aircraft dropping positions

☀ Flares

☆ Torpedo explosions

⚲ Barrage balloons

××××××× Anti-torpedo nets

↙ A/A Guns

C. San Vito